Taste the Sweetness Later

Two Muslim Women in America

Advance Praise for Taste the Sweetness Later

"*Connie Shoemaker expertly recounts the sagas of two strong and resilient women who arrive as refugees after leaving all they know behind. We learn to admire their tremendous effort to adapt as Shoemaker brings this struggle to life. This book is wonderfully written, full of humanity, and heartfelt—a potent antidote to the rising nativism that now engulfs America*".

Helen Thorpe
Award-winning author of
The Newcomers: Finding Refuge, Friendship and Hope in an American Classroom

"*These are very personal stories which resonate into larger cultural and global events. Shoemaker works back and forth between the harrowing stories of Nisren and Eman, the history of conflict in the Middle East, and her personal experiences and reflections as a veteran teacher and seasoned traveler. We get to know the people beneath customs that are very different from ours, providing a moving portrait of human beings negotiating the perilous territory of personal life-choices and societal constraints in war time. We watch as they struggle to maintain their sense of self and social continuity in the face of chaos and tyranny.*"

Mark A. Clarke
Professor Emeritus, University of Colorado Denver
Author of *Common Ground, Contested Territory and A Place to Stand*

"Taste the Sweetness, Connie Shoemaker's warm and intimate story of two remarkable Muslim women living in Colorado, moved me in deep and unexpected ways. It's disturbing to read of the very real pain and fear that war and dictatorship inflicted on these women and their families. It is also hard to read of the homesickness, poverty, bias, and cultural and political barriers they have encountered here. Yet in the end, this is a heartwarming story of resilience, and of the women's determination to safeguard their children and to learn, grow and adapt to new lives. Like the millions of immigrant women who have come before them to these "Golden Shores," they are making America a stronger, better country."

Susan Thornton
Former Littleton Mayor
Founder and Chair, Immigrant Pathways Colorado

"What is it like living under a dictator, Saddam or Qaddafi, and, when you think you're safe, facing the challenges of a female Muslim immigrant in the United States? Connie Shoemaker brings us into the world of two strong women struggling to secure a future with education, peace, and freedom for their children. They sacrifice to Taste the Sweetness Later."

Patricia Ann Paul
Author of *Interesting Times: A Vietnam-Era Memoir*

"Connie Shoemaker's poignant, poetic narration of the journeys of two uprooted Muslim women—one from Iraq, the other from Libya—to a new life in America reminds us that what is often overlooked in the 24/7 news cycle's breathless reports of global and political upheavals—war, invasion, occupation—is the terrible human cost of these calamities. Taste the Sweetness Later puts a memorable and profoundly human face on the turbulent geopolitical times we live in"

George Bilgere
Pushcart Prize-winning author of *Blood Pages*.

"In this beautifully written, highly engaging account, Connie Shoemaker follows the journeys of two women who have been forced to leave their home countries of Iraq and Libya. As their stories unfold, the reader not only gains insight into the difficulties that both Nisren and Eman have to deal with but also witnesses their incredible strength and determination as they face enormous challenges. One hopes that this book will dispel any previously held stereotypes of Muslim women."

Susan Polycarpou
Former Academic Coordinator, Spring International Language Center
Co-author of *In the News and Write Ideas*

"Shoemaker undertook a monumental task and completed it with clarity. Her hours of interviews, careful research, detailed descriptions, and keen understanding of the Arab world provide information, insight, and inspiration, while her vivid imagery piques interest."

Lois Tschetter Hjelmstad,
Author of *Abidance: A Memoir of Love and Inevitability*

"Taste the Sweetness Later exemplifies the extraordinary learning that comes from hearing others' stories and reflecting on how those stories echo in our own. Taste the Sweetness Later: Two Muslim Women in America offers an intimate look at the stories of two women in their own words that tell of their challenges, dreams and hopes in coming to America. Their voices ring true with a sense of the familiar. Readers can recognize themselves in these stories of making choices that are difficult, but which offer promise for a better future. In today's times, these voices and stories remind us that core values of love, sacrifice, and family are shared by all and that making room in our lives for hearing others' stories is worth the effort."

Jeanne Hind,
Director Emerita, Spring International Language Center, Denver
Co-author *Ready to Read (Oxford University Press)*

ALSO BY CONNIE SHOEMAKER

The Good Daughter:
Secrets, Life Stories, and Healing

"Ma'alesh: Verses from Egypt"

Write in the Corner Where You Are, Write in the Middle,
Interactive Techniques for the ESL Class Room

Co-author of *Write Ideas and Inside the News*

Taste the Sweetness Later

Two Muslim Women in America

CONNIE SHOEMAKER

TASTE THE SWEETNESS LATER:
Two Muslim Women In America

Print ISBN: 978-0-9864253-8-7   EISBN: 978-0-9864253-9-4

Library of Congress Control Number: 2018910787

Taste The Sweetness Later™ is an Amity Bridge Books trademark.

Names: Shoemaker, Connie, author.
Title: Taste the sweetness later : two Muslim women in America /
Connie Shoemaker.
Description: Littleton, Colorado : Amity Bridge Books, [2019]
Identifiers: ISBN 9780986425387 (print) I ISBN 9780986425394 (ebook)
Subjects: LCSH: Muslim women--United States--Biography. I Muslim
women--United States--Social conditions. I Women refugees--United
States--Biography. I Women--Libya--Social conditions. I
Women--Iraq--Social conditions. I LCGFT: Biographies.
Classification: LCC HQ1170 .S46 2019 (print) I LCC HQ1170 (ebook) I DDC
305.486970973--dc23

Cover and Interior Design: Cindi Yaklich Epicenter Creative, LLC

"Belief in the power of storytelling can inspire us, make us think differently about the world around us, and help us open our minds and hearts to others."

~ Michelle Obama

MY DEEP APPRECIATION:

To my colleague, Pambos, with gratitude for forty years of sharing
the adventure of educating students from around the world.

Author's Note: Some of the names of people and places have been changed to protect their identity.
More than 200 hours of interviews have allowed Nisren and Eman to tell their stories in their own
words with only minor edits for clarity.

CONTENTS

PART I   NISREN

PART II   EMAN

Introduction

I FIRST MET NISREN, HER HUSBAND RAAD, AND TWO CHILDREN IN AUGUST 2009 THE MORNING AFTER THEY ARRIVED IN DENVER, COLORADO, AFTER AN EXHAUSTING TWENTY-FIVE HOUR TRIP FROM BAGHDAD, IRAQ. As a board member of a new nonprofit organization whose goal was to help integrate immigrants into the community, I had joined two other board members, Susan Thornton and Mika Farer, to welcome our first immigrant family. Susan, a former two-time mayor of Littleton, Colorado, had received a plea for help from US Army Colonel Joe Rice, a Colorado State House Representative on leave for his third tour of duty in Iraq. Colonel Rice knew Nisren's husband Raad in his role as an official interpreter for the US Army and was aware of the death threats that faced him and his family in Baghdad. Anti-American sentiment had grown when the US-led coalition had toppled dictator Saddam Hussein. Baghdad had become a major center for resistance against the occupiers with an estimated 1200 local interpreters severely injured and 360 interpreters killed between the beginning of the war and the so-called "surge" in 2007. Colonel Rice offered to sponsor the family's immigration to his home state under the Special Immigrant Visa (SIV), which was available to Iraqi and Afghan translators and interpreters working for the US military. He asked Susan to arrange for our group to meet the family at the airport, find housing, secure a job for Raad and, in general, assist them in their adjustment to life in Colorado, a place they had never heard of before.

This was a tall order for a new organization with only a few board members. Because I had spent many years of my professional life welcoming international students to the intensive "English as a second language" (ESL) program I had co-founded, I volunteered to welcome the family at Denver International Airport and take them to the motel I had booked. I held my welcome sign with the family's name above my head as we scanned the hundreds of arrivals coming up the escalator into the main floor of the terminal. During the thirty minutes we waited, no identifiable family of four emerged into the waiting area. After checking the baggage claim area, we asked the airline to confirm their status and found they had missed their flight from Washington, DC, and would arrive four hours later. The airline offered to contact Raad with the name of the motel and the message that I would meet them in the morning.

A handsome, smiling family greeted me in the motel lobby the next day. They had just come back from a stroll around the tree-lined neighborhood near the motel, the first walk they had ever taken as a family without the fear of being followed.

Raad immediately stepped forward to firmly shake my hand. His height, about six-foot-three, broad shoulders, and muscular arms confirmed his take-charge attitude. He had a close-cropped army-style haircut and a neatly-trimmed black moustache and short beard. With a sweep of his arm, he introduced Nisren and the two children. I guessed that he was the only one who spoke English, so I welcomed them in the Arabic I had learned in the four years my family had spent in Cairo, Egypt, with the hope that I would make Nisren and the children feel more comfortable.

I was drawn to Nisren's face, made the focal point by her light green *hijab*, a scarf that covered her hair, fastened under her chin, and spread over her shoulders. Warmth and joy radiated from her hazel eyes and gentle, slightly dimpled smile. Our hand shake turned into a hug with a light touch on each cheek. She smoothed the skirt of her dark green, long-sleeved *abaya* and said, "*Shukran*. Thank you." Years later, she told me how relieved she was on their arrival in Colorado. "The Colorado air smelled beautiful. It was like breathing life," Nisren said in her best English. "That was the first time I had slept through the night for six years; the first time I hadn't worried about danger to my family. In Iraq, my ears were like rabbit ears. I was always listening for someone trying to open the door that we barricaded every night."

Linking arms with her mother was Noor, an adorable, shy ten-year-old dressed American-style in blue jeans and a red, short-sleeved top with her black hair pulled back from her high forehead in a braid that almost reached her waist. Blue sandals that matched her brother's completed her outfit. Nisren gave her a gentle push forward to greet me. Noor politely stretched out her hand, eyes cast down, for me to shake. Eight-year-old Mohammed had a "me, too!" look on his face as he grabbed my other hand and waited for a hug. He could have been an American first-grader with his cropped jeans and white tee with the word "Garage" and automobile emblems on it. The wavy black hair that fell over his forehead contrasted with his dad's crew cut.

My friendship with Nisren and her family continued through the ups and downs of their lives as immigrants. I began toying with the idea that Nisren's life story should be shared in a book. She had survived childhood hardships as part of Saddam Hussein's discrimination against the Kurdish minority in Iraq in addition to death threats after Raad signed on as an English language interpreter working with the US military in Baghdad. Her courage and resilience were note-worthy both in her life at home and in her new life in the United States.

At this point in my life, I was Director Emerita of Spring International Language Center in Littleton, Colorado, the intensive ESL program that I co-founded in 1979. I was semi-retired but unable to leave behind the diversity of student cultures and the collegiality and friendship of the instructors and staff. Each nine-week term, I had the privilege of welcoming and introducing new students at an orientation meeting. In the cultural sea of faces at the October 2013 orientation, my attention was immediately drawn to a young woman in a rose- and blue-flowered head scarf framing laughing brown eyes and a broad smile. My thirty-plus years of working with students from the Middle East and North Africa had honed my cultural identification skills. I guessed that this vivacious young lady was from Libya, a country whose hard-working, bright Muslim students had impressed me since 1977 when I had recently returned from Egypt and had begun teaching international students in Denver. When I introduced myself, she responded with a firm handshake, a direct gaze, and "I'm Eman from Libya. Happy to meet you."

During the ensuing weeks of the term, the good vibes about Eman were part of her teachers' informal conversations. They praised her intellectual curiosity, poise, grace, sense of humor, determination, and willingness to mentor other students. Her fans at the school were even more amazed when they learned she was from a family of twenty-three children. Just eighteen months before her arrival, the Libyan Revolution had burst into a full-blown Arab Spring. Eman, her husband Sami, and sixteen-month-old Saif, born on the day the revolution began, had left behind a life punctuated by bombs and artillery fire, no electricity, and very little water for "an adventure in the United States," as she called it. She had received a scholarship from the Libyan government two years earlier but hadn't obtained the required F-1 student visa until June 2013. Sami was allowed to come with her on an F-2 visa as an accompanying spouse but was not permitted to work. He was staying home to care for their son while his wife completed English and her goal of a master's degree in computer science.

Eman breezed through the upper levels of our academic English program and delivered a graduation speech that emphasized hard work and achieving goals. I pushed her story to the back of my mind for two years until she graduated from the University of Colorado at Denver and was invited back to encourage students as the speaker at another Spring International graduation. Seeing her with her prized mortarboard perched atop her brightly-colored hijab gave me the incentive I needed to write her story, coupled with Nisren's. Putting their lives side by side would allow readers to know them as individuals but to also see the similarities they shared as members of the same faith who had to adjust to new lives in a strikingly different culture. Both were devout Muslim women whose lives were structured by the rules of their religion from the way they dressed to their arranged marriages. Outwardly, their dress was similar: a hijab hair covering and a long-sleeved, full-length dress or cloak. Nisren was Shiite, and Eman was Sunni, representing the two major denominations of Islam. Both had lived their entire lives in countries led by murderous dictators. However, their goals in coming to the US were quite different. Nisren was a refugee who escaped from her country, and Eman was an international student who came to the United States for higher education. These differences shaped their lives in the ensuing years. Most importantly, their stories encompass values that all women share: love of family, close relationships with their husbands, education to better their own and their children's lives, and the freedom to make individual choices.

An even more compelling reason to share these stories is the hope of bridging the social and political chasm dividing America today.

Fear of persons of a different skin color, religion, dress, or political party has burst into a flood of hatred that has damaged the paths that should connect us and is being used by those who would divide us. The Muslim community is one of the major targets of this fear.

Just as knowledge frees us and makes us more able to function correctly, ignorance condemns us to the bondage of fear. *Taste the Sweetness* chips away at ignorance by giving readers the opportunity to become intimately acquainted with two Muslim women through the life stories they tell.

Nisren and Eman display the courage, determination, and unwavering hope that are essential to the true spirit of America. Their stories serve as inspiration for anyone who faces difficult and seemingly insurmountable hardships. The wisdom of Eman's sheepherding grandmother sums it up: "Swallow it now, and you will taste the sweetness later."

Part I

Nisren

Historical Backdrop: Iraq from 1979 to 2014

1979: Nisren's birth. Saddam Hussein, a secularist who rose to power in the Sunni Ba'ath political party, takes over as president of Iraq.

1980: Iraq launches an air attack against Iran, beginning the Iran-Iraq war. Saddam Hussein claims his reason for the invasion is a territorial dispute over Shatt al-Arab, the waterway which forms the boundary between the two countries.

1988: The Iran-Iraq war ends in a stalemate with an estimated 1.8 million Iraqis dead in the conflict. Saddam retaliates against the Kurds for supporting Iran and uses poison gas to kill Kurds in Halabja in northern Iraq. Thousands of people are believed to have died in the attack.

1990: Iraq invades Kuwait. Saddam justifies the attack by blaming Kuwait for falling oil prices that harm the Iraqi economy. The United Nations (UN) imposes economic sanctions and issues a Security Council resolution setting January 15, 1991 as the deadline for Iraq's withdrawal from Kuwait.

1991: Operation Desert Storm is launched in January after Iraq fails to comply with the UN resolution. The Persian Gulf War is led by the US and a coalition of thirty-two countries under the leadership of US General Norman Schwarzkopf. Air strikes on Baghdad begin. By February, ground forces have vanquished the Iraqi army and freed Kuwait. In April, a formal cease-fire is signed and Saddam Hussein accepts the UN resolution agreeing to destroy weapons of mass destruction and allow UN inspectors to monitor the disarmament. Economic and financial sanctions continue until 2003.

1992: The US launches cruise missiles on Baghdad after Saddam attempts to assassinate US president George H W Bush when he visits Kuwait.

1995: The UN Security Council establishes an "oil-for-food: program, providing Iraq with the opportunity to sell oil to finance the purchase of humanitarian goods. Iraq does not accept the plan.

1998: Nisren and Raad's marriage. Great Britain and the US launch air strikes against Iraq. The attack, called Operation Desert Fox, is in response to Iraq's refusal to cooperate with UN weapons inspectors.

2000: Noor's birth.

2001: After the September 11 terrorist attacks on the US, President George W. Bush begins calling for a "regime change" in Iraq, describing the nation as part of an "axis of evil."

2002: Mohammed's birth. Facing the threat of US air strikes, Iraq unconditionally agrees to the return of UN weapons inspectors. The Iraqi Foreign Minister sends a letter to the UN from Saddam Hussein stating that Iraq has no chemical, nuclear or biological weapons. The UN Security Council outlines strict new weapons inspections and threatens "serious consequences" if Iraq fails to comply. Iraq agrees to comply. UN inspectors begin working in Iraq and find "little or no" evidence of weapons of mass destruction.

2003: In spite of the "no evidence" report, in March a US-led coalition invades Iraq and topples Saddam Hussein's government marking the start of years of violent conflict with different groups competing for power.

2003: Raad becomes an interpreter for the US Marines. In April, Baghdad surrenders to the US armed forces, and Iraq is occupied. As many as 85,000 Ba'athist party members lose their jobs as a result of a Coalition Provisional Authority (CPA) order. Anti-US sentiment begins. In September, Saddam Hussein is captured in an underground bunker near Tikrit.

2004: Radical Shiite cleric Muqtada al-Sadr, who had demanded withdrawal of all coalition troops, sends his militia to attack military and CPA installations. Suicide bombers attack Shiite festivals in Baghdad and Karbala, killing 140 people.

The US hands over sovereignty to an interim government headed by Prime Minister Iyad Allawi.

2005: Iraqis vote for the first full-term government and parliament since the US-led invasion.

2006: A tribunal finds Saddam Hussein guilty for crimes against humanity, and he is hanged.

2007: US President Bush announces a new Iraq strategy; thousands more US troops will be dispatched to shore up security in Baghdad.

Refugee resettlement to the US and other countries begins.

2008: The Iraqi Parliament approves a security pact with the US under which all US troops are due to leave the country by the end of 2011. They also pass legislation allowing former officials from Saddam Hussein's Ba'athist party to return to public life.

2009: The family immigrates to the US. Newly inaugurated US President Barack Obama announces withdrawal of 12,000 US troops by the end of August 2010. Up to 50,000 will stay on until the end of 2011 to advise Iraqi forces and protect US interests.

2012: Hussein's birth.

2014: The family becomes US citizens.

CHAPTER I

"Eyes Are on Us"

THE HOT, DRY BAGHDAD AIR IN THE ONE-BEDROOM APARTMENT CONSUMED
ELEVEN-YEAR-OLD NISREN AS SHE CURLED UP ON THE SOFA BED TRYING
TO SLEEP AWAY A STOMACHACHE THAT HAD KEPT HER HOME FROM SCHOOL.
Her long brown hair was plaited in a loose braid lying across the
shoulder of her blue shift. Beads of perspiration glistened on her
forehead and threaded down her flushed cheeks. Filling her nostrils
was the comforting smell of *khubuz tannour* bread dough baking
in the cylindrical clay oven. Her mother's rhythmic slapping and
kneading of another batch of dough lulled her into sleep. Hopefully,
their neighbors would buy the newly-baked flatbread prepared by
her mother. Every child over ten years of age and every adult in the
family of nine was focused on earning money for their food and the
tiny apartment. Enas, Senna, and Sara, Nisren's younger sisters, and
Samir and Wanir, her little brothers, were in school today. Her sight-
impaired father and the baby of the family, Venos, were sleeping in
the bedroom. Her eldest brother, Munir, had paid for an excuse from
army duty, so he could work three days a week in a shoe factory.
Economic and political restrictions were part of the family's daily
lives as Kurds, an ethnic minority in Iraq persecuted by tyrant
Saddam Hussein's Ba'athist government.

It was October of 1991, one of the worst years of deprivation caused by the economic ravages of Saddam, who had oppressed Iraq for more than twelve years. He had unleashed devastating regional wars and reduced his once promising, oil-rich nation to a claustrophobic police state. The family's security, food, housing, and employment were directly affected by United Nations (UN) sanctions placed on the country after Saddam's invasion of Kuwait a year ago. Nisren was used to living without many necessities in life, but the lack of work for her older brothers and inability of her father to work had forced the family to continually move to smaller apartments in poverty-stricken areas of Baghdad. Added to the bare-bones lifestyle was fear for their very existence. Just six months earlier, Nisren and her family had fled from the apartment to a basement shelter in response to air-attack alarms. The US-led coalition, Operation Desert Storm, was bombing Baghdad in an attempt to end the war with Kuwait.

Nisren had just dozed off when screams and pounding on the door of the apartment above startled her awake.

"Mama, what was that?"

"Just stay where you are and be quiet," her mother whispered, wiping her hands on her apron as she walked toward the hallway door that had been left ajar because of the heat. Before she reached the door, two teenage boys from the upstairs apartment flung the door wide open as they scurried into the apartment to hide. One of the boys stumbled into the unlit toilet room and the other slammed the apartment door behind him and crouched on the floor next to the sofa bed where Nisren was startled awake. She sat up, clutching her hands together on her lap. She looked down in amazement at the neighbor boy who had rolled himself into a ball with his head between his arms. Within minutes, two men wearing the grey uniforms of Saddam Hussein's secret police kicked aside the door.

"There's one of them!" shouted a short, fat man as he spotted the boy hiding next to the sofa bed. He grabbed him by the arm, twisted it behind him, and yanked him to his feet.

"You," he said to Nisren's mom. "Where's the other motherfucker?"

Her eyes swept the room and, turning to Nisren, she whispered in Kurdish, "Tell them the other boy isn't here."

Nisren considered the consequences of lying to the thugs. She remained seated and with respectfully down-turned eyes, said in Arabic, "I don't know. I just woke up. It's just Mama and me, and my father and the baby asleep in the bedroom."

The second man, sporting a square, bristly Saddam-style moustache, began searching the apartment, first the bedroom where he confronted Nisren's father, who could barely see the shadowy figure of the man, and a startled, whimpering baby who was awakened by the noise. Not finding the offender there, he went on to the bathroom and peered into the darkness. He did not see the boy pressed against the wall behind the door, so he rejoined his colleague, who was slapping the terrified teen's face as he held him by the hair. Blood was dripping from the boy's nose.

"Where's your brother? Where is he?" he said between slaps. "You're supposed to be in the army, both of you."

The boy was crying so hard, he couldn't answer. The thug with the moustache gave him a punch in the stomach that made him crumple to the floor.

"*Khalas.* Finished! You're coming with us," he said as he jerked him to his feet.

Before they turned to leave, they asked Nisren if there were older brothers in the family. She replied that her eldest brother, Munir, was nineteen, and he was at work in a shoe factory, wisely adding that he had an official excuse from the army to work three days a week and report for army duty the other two days.

With a nod of satisfaction, the short man coughed, spat into his hand, and wiped it on his trousers. They grabbed the struggling boy by his shoulders, brushed past her mother and marched out of the apartment. When they were gone, Nisren and her mama, trembling from the frightening experience, sank down on the sofa and embraced each other. The floor in front of them was covered with blood and hair. A piece of chewing gum was stuck in the drying blood. Nisren went into the bathroom and told the trembling boy to stay there until they were certain Saddam's thugs were gone. Then she and mama used rags and soapy water to clean the floor before the children came home from school.

The visit from Saddam's thugs was not an isolated incidence. Maybe once or twice a week, someone in the apartment building would be frightened by a barrage of banging on the door with the message, "I've come for your husband, your son." The Arab and Christian neighbors in the apartment building were always protective of the Kurdish family when authorities tried to gather information about them. "They are good people. They never say anything bad about Saddam Hussein. They love him," was their standard answer.

It was six years after the family had immigrated to the US. Nisren and I were sitting on adjoining sofas in the spotless living room of the family's small duplex in Littleton, Colorado. The mini-blinds were always closed, but the flickering TV, tuned to Arabic cartoons, and the window in the kitchen provided some light. On the wall over the sofa was a woven tapestry with artistic Arabic calligraphy recording one of Prophet Muhammad's sayings about seeking refuge from evil. Fourteen-year-old Mohammed and sixteen-year-old Noor were in school. Hussein, who was not quite three, would rather show me his plastic action figure than watch the cartoon. His newly-trimmed black hair had a wavy lock that fell over his forehead. I forgot the running voice recorder sitting on the end table between Nisren and me and paid attention to the swoops and shouts of Spider Man as Hussein raced around the room. Nisren's bare feet peaked out from under the black abaya that matched the hijab that covered her hair. She patiently settled her beloved third child on the sofa and turned to me. With one arm around Hasooni, her term of endearment for him, she leaned forward, eager to tell me more.

"I just remembered another time when Saddam's people came to our house, but I was only three or four years old." She paused to knit together her childhood memory with her parents' account of the event.

"It was cold, and I was in my night clothes. My aunt grabbed me up in a jacket to protect me, and we were put in a truck. Women and children were crying. They took us to a government building where there were hundreds of people. We were separated by family name and put into a room that was so small the adults had to stand up shoulder to shoulder."

The round-up of Shiites, who represent sixty to sixty-five percent of Muslims in Iraq, and Kurdish people of Iranian descent was an infamous part of the Iran-Iraq conflict. The conflict consisted of three back-to-back wars waged by Saddam after he had risen to power and taken over the Ba'ath Party as President in 1979, the same year that Nisren was born. Shiites form one of the two great branches of Islam. About 150 million Shiites are spread around the world, most of them in Iran, Iraq, India, and Pakistan. While the Sunni branch makes up the greater part of the global Muslim population of more than a billion, Shiites form the majority in Iraq—as many as fifteen million out of a population of twenty-four million. However, they have never held power in Iraq nor fully participated in its government and at times have been brutally repressed. Not only was Nisren's family Shiite, they were also Kurdish, a non-Arabic, mostly Sunni Muslim people with their own language and culture. The Kurds supported Iran in the Iran-Iraq War, so they were targeted in the round-up that Nisren remembered.

Nisren gently rubbed Hussein's back as she searched her mind for more details about the night her family was loaded into a truck and taken away from her childhood home. "I was told that every adult in that room was asked the same question: 'Are you from Iran or Iraq?'"

Luckily, two family members on her father's side could verify they were originally from Iraq with documents they had carried with them into the interrogation room. "People who had Iranian roots were kicked out of the country without any of their clothes, food, or possessions," according to Nisren. "If they were Iranian, they were told to leave the country." Saddam's forces continued to abduct Kurds and Shiítes to demand proof that they did not sympathize with Iranian Shiítes. If their claims were unsatisfactory, they were either executed or forced out of Iraq.

Nisren remembered changes in their neighborhood in the days after the round-up. "I saw that some of my Kurdish friends and their families were missing. My parents later told me that their houses were rented or sold and that some of the people had been killed."

She glanced over at me for reassurance that I had understood her description of that night. The tension around her eyes as she described the round-up had eased into relief. It seemed that sharing this frightening chapter of her childhood story had placed it appropriately in the past where it belonged. Hussein slid from her side and plopped down in front of the TV screen. I was silent as I thought about the impact of these events on Nisren and her family. How could they go on with their daily lives when a knock on the door could signal torture, imprisonment, or even the end of their lives? How much fear of reprisal would it take to say you love the murderous leader of your country when you despise him? That kind of naked fear was never part of my childhood as a white, middle-class kid in west Denver. But, unfortunately, it had recently impacted my teen-age granddaughters' lives as a result of school shootings in the US, starting in my own Columbine High School neighborhood and spreading across the country. After these events, students in the US began to look over their shoulders with fear, and their parents no longer felt safe sending their children to school. Fear, I realized, can be perpetuated in any culture or country.

My eyes met Nisren's. She smiled and leaned forward on the sofa. Rather than thinking about the sadness in her own life, she was thinking about me. My face must have reflected the shock and empathy I felt after listening to her story. To reassure me, she said, "Don't worry. Connie. I have some good memories as a kid, too." As our interviews progress, I learned that the shared Arab and American adage "Every cloud has as silver lining" was woven into Nisren's approach to her life experiences. She always tried to balance the frightening events in her life with pleasant outcomes.

"When I was really little, we all lived together in rented apartments in a big building with a garden. Saddam's Ba'athist regime didn't allow Kurds to buy property, so we had to rent. Aunt Warda, my dad's sister, took care of me until I was about six years old. She lived on the first floor of the apartment building, and my parents lived on the second floor while my grandparents took the elevator to their third floor rooms."

"Why weren't you staying with your mom on the second floor?"

"My mom tried to get me to move up to the second floor to be closer to her, but my aunt wanted to take care of me because her kids were grown up. I loved to be with her."

Her favorite aunt, whom she described as "tall, strong, and older than her father" would take her every morning at 6:30 or 7 to shop for the day. They visited the grocery, the bakery, and the meat market. All the shopkeepers recognized Nisren, kissed her cheeks, and gave her sweets.

"I loved all the attention," she said, "but Aunt Warda had strict rules." Because her children were in college and had to study, she only allowed Nisren to watch TV for an hour or less, so the house would be quiet. Nisren could not go outside to play with other kids, but in the afternoon, Aunt Warda would have a tea party with her in the garden. In the evening, Nisren's father would return from work at a printing press, shower, and take the children, only three of them at this point, to play in a park where there were children from Yemen, Egypt, and Sudan with their parents who worked in Iraq. Sometimes he would take them to dinner in a restaurant.

She had a catch in her voice as she talked about her father.

"I was my father's little girl. When Baba would get mad at my mom and didn't want to eat with anyone, she would say, 'You go talk to him.' We always talked and cooked together. He loved the kitchen and made a mess, but I cleaned up after him."

Her father was lucky to be alive. As a young man, he had lived in the Kurdish north fighting along with the Kurdish army. Saddam captured the fighters and either put them in jail or executed them. For some reason unknown to Nisren, her father was spared and allowed to go back to Baghdad where he married her mother. Neither one of them had the opportunity to go to school.

As the family and the cost of housing grew, her father made the decision to move from the large apartment building to another neighborhood. No matter where they lived, the children were protected from the dangers of the outside world by limiting their freedom to leave their home. Nisren's mother had a firm schedule for after school. The children would come home, have a snack if there was enough food, do their homework, and then take a nap. When they lived in the two-room apartment that Saddam's thugs invaded, there was only one bathroom with a shower for all the families on the floor, so showers had to be scheduled every other day before nap time. Mama enforced their quiet time by popping her head in the doorway of the bedroom when she heard giggling or talking.

"She would look at us like this," Nisren said as she wrinkled her brow and narrowed her eyes, "and wave her slipper like she was going to give us a swat if we didn't be quiet." Hussein, who was curled up in the crook of her arm, laughed at the face she made.

These were empty threats because neither of her parents believed in physical punishment. Another part of the routine was the strict two-hour time limit on their outdoor play. Instead of calling them in when their time was up, she gave each of the older children a wrist watch, so they would know when to come in.

"I was in sixth grade when my mom gave me my watch," Nisren recalled. "I was so proud that she trusted me to use it." Along with the watch came several warnings: "Don't go past the apartment house next door. Don't listen to any talk about Saddam, and don't bring any talk back from the street to the house. No conversation or bad words. Our family doesn't use those."

Her pleasant childhood memories quickly slipped into more difficult reminiscences.

When her father lost his job at the printing press because his eyesight was failing, lack of money forced the family to make a third move to a cheaper place in a different neighborhood where there were Christian, Jewish, and Arab Muslim families with many children. They rented individual rooms in an older apartment building. Even more than ever before, fear invaded their lives. Through the grapevine, her family was aware of frequent visits to the neighborhood from Saddam's henchmen.

"I always had to remember that 'Eyes were on us,'" she recalled. This phrase was like a billboard in her mind as she traveled through her early elementary school days and on to adulthood. Along with the image of piercing eyes were the repeated cautions: Don't talk to strangers. Don't tell any of your school friends about your parents and what they say at home. They might go home and tell their parents and then we'd be in trouble. Remember when someone asks you about Saddam, you must say "We love Saddam."

Spying targeted more than the Kurdish population. Every Iraqi was spied on, even those who were part of the Ba'athist regime. Paranoia was part of everyday life. A person could be spied on by neighbors, work colleagues, fellow students at university, even by guests at weddings and funerals.

"I remember that my father was concerned about going to the mosque too often because spies might think he was meeting someone against the regime or listening too much to a religious sheikh who was fomenting revolt. He decided to go once a week, pray, and leave quickly, so there would be no suspicions about him."

The Ba'athist supposedly "secret" service headquarters was next door to the children's school. Her father was frequently approached by members saying, "Come to our meetings. We'll give you money." He knew that he would be asked to spy on other Kurds and would be targeted if he said a direct "No" to these requests, so he would go to a meeting and then have excuses about injuries or sickness when they asked again. Scrutiny of Kurds in Baghdad increased in 1988 when the Iraq-Iran War ended in a stalemate. Saddam's air force, in retaliation for Kurdish support of Iran, dropped poison gas on Kurdish towns and villages in the north. When the campaign ended in 1989, ninety percent of Kurdish villages had been wiped off the map and up to 100,000 people had been slaughtered.

Even schools were infiltrated by junior spies. "In elementary school, I didn't quite understand that 'the eyes' were Saddam's spies, but when I reached middle school, I discovered that the girl leaders would always be listening to hear any bad things that we said about the regime. These were the strong girls, not quiet like me," she said. "They were the ones who raised the flag every Thursday, the last school day of the week, spoke on the microphone, and led us in exercises. They called each other 'sister,' but the rest of us were just 'friends.'"

Being shy was a typical characteristic of Kurdish children who did not want to draw attention to themselves. Nisren did not want to stand out from her classmates, so it was important for her to be fluent in Arabic, although Kurdish, which belongs to the Indo-European language group, was what she heard and spoke at home. Without the benefit of formal education, her father was fluent in both Kurdish and Arabic, but her mother spoke only Kurdish. A few of Nisren's classmates were also Kurdish, but the majority of the students were from varied backgrounds: Her best friend Lillia was Christian, and there were others who were Jewish and Arab Muslims, both Shiite and Sunni.

Teachers were not always kind to Kurdish students. Nisren remembered an embarrassing experience in the fifth grade. Checking homework was an important part of each class. If students didn't have their assignments, they would be struck with a ruler on the backs and fronts of their hands. Although Kurdish was Nisren's native language, she was progressing nicely in Arabic, the major language of Iraq. Her Arabic teacher, Abdul Latif, asked her to put her homework on the blackboard or she would not receive points for it. Everyone was watching her as she walked to the front of the classroom and picked up the chalk. She painstakingly copied the sentences in neat Arabic letters with all the correct grammar. When she finished, Abdul Latif made her stay at the blackboard. "Just look at that," he said. "She must have been in a hurry to get home for lunch. No spaces here and here. She's running together." He laughed and pointed at the way

Nisren had formatted her sentences. The students laughed with him. She hung her head and hurried to sit down.

"I'd rather be punished with a ruler than made fun of," she told me. "A ruler is quick, and no one remembers or talks about it." Although this bad memory was never erased, her Arabic teacher in the next grade "was wonderful" and gave her praise when she did well. "I loved school and wanted to continue, but I was worried because many difficult things were happening around us, and my mother needed me at home."

CHAPTER 2

Hungry and Uprooted

In 1991, when Nisren was eleven, the Gulf War, called Operation Desert Storm in the United States, was waged by coalition forces from thirty-five nations led by the US against Iraq in response to Iraq's invasion and annexation of neighboring Kuwait. The combat phase only lasted from January 17 to February 28 when a formal cease-fire was signed. Saddam accepted United Nations (UN) resolution 687 agreeing to stop Iraq from building nuclear, chemical, or biological weapons and to allow UN inspectors to monitor the disarmament.

The end of the Iraq-Kuwait war did not mean that life for families like Nisren's improved. In fact, it grew worse. Economic sanctions were put in place to prevent Saddam from threatening the region by rebuilding his army and producing weapons of mass destruction. The strongest of these sanctions were limits on oil exports. Oil provided money for everything from the availability of food to adequate medical services. In addition to this hardship, UN Security Council sanctions banned all trade and financial resources, exempting medicine, some foodstuffs, and certain "humanitarian circumstances." The embargoes lasted a devastating twelve years. According to David Rieff, writing in the *New York Times Magazine* in 2003, opponents of these sanctions insisted that the restrictions "transformed a country that in the 1980s was the envy of the developing world in terms of investments in health, education and physical infrastructure into a place where everyone (except the half-million or so members of Saddam Hussein's Ba'ath Party and their families and cronies) was dependent on United Nations food aid, where infant mortality rates had skyrocketed, educational outcomes had collapsed and diseases that had disappeared were reappearing, sometimes at epidemic levels....Several hundred thousand children who could reasonably have been expected to live, died before their fifth birthdays."

Lack of food was a daily concern for Nisren's family. The Iraqi government offered free food rations consisting of 1,000 calories per person per day, which was only forty percent of the daily nutritional requirements. It was estimated that sixty percent of the population relied on these handouts. Regime loyalists, the wealthy Iraqis, were able to continue their lives of abundance while Nisren's mother stood in line for hours at the market to buy poor quality flour, some canned goods, and cooking oil. Many families experienced high rates of malnutrition, lack of medical supplies, and diseases from lack of clean water, the 1993 United Nations Children's Fund (UNICEF) reported.

Obligations to house extended family members and continued lack of income increased the burden on Nisren's family. When her grandparents, in addition to an uncle and aunt, did not have enough money to rent a place of their own, her father and older brother decided to leave the tiny apartment to find a larger place. They located an old house that could barely hold the family that had grown to thirteen people. They built up the low walls to make them high enough "to keep us safe from thieves, kidnapping, and killing." The house had a living room, which they used as a bedroom at night, a bedroom, a kitchen, and a bathroom. At night, the men slept on the living room floor, and the women and children slept in the bedroom.

"When my dad's parents moved in with us, they sold their refrigerator and stove to help pay for food for the family," she said. Her mother also sold some antique plates and other items to help them buy necessities. "We never had enough money for fruit, fresh vegetables, or meat. Sometimes we ate only once, lunch at 4 p.m., so we wouldn't feel hungry before going to sleep early."

Nisren thought of this time with a mix of sadness and familial closeness. "Because there weren't enough blankets for everyone, my sister Enas and I always slept curled up together on top of a sheet on the floor with her on one side and my younger brother on the other side to keep each other warm. We've always felt a special, strong connection since those difficult times. Even today, when I need to talk to someone, Enas is always there. She knows everything about me."

As I parked in front of the family's duplex in Littleton for another interview, I imagined Nisren's thirteen family members packed into a house half its size. After spending several years in a two-bedroom apartment waiting for a larger rental subsidized by the City of Littleton, the family reached the top of the long list of applicants. In order to qualify for affordable housing, Nisren agreed to spend five hours a month volunteering in the community. She chose to work at her beloved Bemis Library in Littleton where she had studied English.

It was 11 a.m. on a sunny Tuesday in April 2016. Some tulip bulbs Noor had planted in the fall were poking their green leaves through the clay soil on each side of the cracked concrete sidewalk leading to the duplex. A garden bench with peeling brown paint was sitting forlornly on the porch. The last family to occupy the house probably had left it there. There was no use for it at this time. Sitting on it would draw attention to the occupants of the duplex and might provoke anti-Muslim reaction from neighbors or passersby. As I knocked on the locked screen door, I could smell fresh Iraqi bread.

Nisren unlocked the inside door and the screen door and welcomed me into the living room with a big smile and a hug, instinctively locking the doors behind us. Hussein shyly tiptoed up to me for his greeting hug and then ran to get his latest action figure purchased at the Savers store nearby. Nisren's appreciation of her modest house in Colorado was evident in the meticulous care she took of each room and each piece of furniture. She and Hussein enjoyed my visits as much as I did. Her loneliness was eased by our conversations, and her experiences affirmed by simply telling me about them. Unfortunately, there was no Iraqi community in the Littleton suburb where we had helped them settle. Most Iraqis lived in apartment housing in the southeast suburb of Aurora, so Nisren had difficulty connecting with other Iraqi families. The fact that she didn't drive also isolated her. Raad approved of her learning to drive but hadn't yet found time or the inclination to teach her.

Before we busied ourselves with the interview, Nisren offered me a glass of pomegranate juice, and I gave three-year-old Hussein a small gift of a pop-up book of dinosaurs. He sat cross-legged on the sofa, leafing through the book, and shouting out his pleasure at recognizing the 3-D *Tyrannosaurus rex* and the *Triceratops*. I turned on the voice recorder, and we returned to the topic of our previous conversation: difficult childhood years in their crowded home in central Baghdad.

One day in the spring of 1991, Nisren's mother was laboring over her daily bread-baking in hopes of selling enough of the staple food to earn money to put at least one meal a day on their family table. She had stood in line for the flour for hours although she knew the ground mixture would be "something you'd feed to animals, not humans." Luckily no fat, which was unavailable in the market, was used in making the bread, just flour, water, salt and yeast. Before putting the rounds of bread on the sides of the clay oven, she placed a tray of rising loaves on a chair in the living room. Nisren's father walked cautiously into the room with his cane, found his favorite chair, and sat down, not realizing that a pan of bread loaves occupied his space. He stood up in dismay with the loaves sticking to his pants. This could have been a laughable incident, but it shocked his wife.

"He's so blind he can't see the bread on the chair," her mother said, weeping.

Until that day, everyone knew that Baba had cataracts on his eyes, but no one thought he was almost totally blind. When the cataracts first appeared, he was working at the printing press in a job that required clear vision. He knew he needed to have the cataracts removed, but he was afraid of going through the surgical process. After his eyesight prevented him from fulfilling his duties at the press, he took a job in construction, working alongside Egyptians and Indians, carrying boards and cement but being paid less than the expatriate workers. In the middle of the Iran-Iraq war, construction work disappeared. Then the eldest son, 20-year-old Munir, became the principal bread-winner in the family. By law, he should have been serving full-time in the army, but in order to provide income for the family, he had saved enough money to purchase black market exemption papers that said he was allowed to work several days a week. These papers had to be renewed each month and more money paid.

The bread incident, which her mother confided to her relatives, led to some relief for Nisren's father. "When my mom's brother heard about my dad's eyes, he gave us money for the surgery. It was so expensive that my dad could have only one eye done," she explained.

When it was time for the school year to start, being able to sustain the family from day to day became more important than sending Nisren to school. She had to drop out of fifth grade to help her mother bake bread and care for the younger children. "Many times there was just enough food, mainly bread, for one meal a day," she recalls. "Besides that, my mother was pregnant, and from 4 a.m. until sundown, she was working with the dough until her hands became cracked and infected so badly that she had to wear gloves. I even had to help her lift the oven cover."

Her mother was distraught when she found out she was pregnant with her eighth child. She confided in her daughter that she had taken some folk medicine to stop the pregnancy, but it hadn't worked. Contraception was permitted but not readily available during the war years, so many pregnancies occurred during the worst of times to bring children into the world. There was no choice but to summon the strength to keep working and accept the pregnancy.

Nisren sighed, pulled a now drowsy Hussein closer to her, and threaded her fingers through his hair. Her mind jumped from the past to thoughts of her aging, diabetic mother whom she hadn't seen for four years. I was reminded that Nisren had continued to fight her difficult-to-control diabetes after the birth of Hussein.

"To have a healthy baby you need vitamins, meat, fruits, and vegetables, but Mama didn't have any of these," she said.

Her mother may not have had the healthy diet needed for a pregnant woman, but she did have the strength and determination that kept the family alive and together during times of desperation. With the help of Munir, who was now the the major bread-winner and decision-maker, the family worked as a team with everyone finding some way to contribute. Munir's employment in the shoe factory helped support the family and added to the small money jar that might be enough later to "buy out" his brother Samir from required army service. Even their six-year-old brother worked as a courier for a next door neighbor involved in the black market. He carried a walkie-talkie between buildings. He was never able to go to school and never learned to read or write. Nisren, Enas, and her mother repaired men's shoes at night to make some money for the younger children's school supplies. On the few occasions when her mother obtained sugar, she would bake cookies for Nisren to sell to neighbor children during play time outside the house.

"We had just a few things left from our past lives that people with more money might like, so we sold them just to buy the basic things we needed. Some of my sisters had torn and tattered clothes but no money to buy new ones. My mom's brother saw this and bought them some new clothes. Her side of the family was able to help us more than my dad's," she explained. "Sometimes when I'd go to bed, I would think about the happy times when I was just a little girl." With a lift of her chin, she recalled those hard times not with sadness, but with a sense of pride at the strength the family showed. "No one in our family died from hunger or sickness like some people in Baghdad."

Her mother managed to get through her pregnancy and give birth to baby Venos, an event that changed Nisren's life. At twelve years of age, she became the care-giver and mother to Venos, whom she adored. "The baby was very weak, so we took her to the hospital for some shots. We realized then how much better she was than the many dying babies we saw there," she said.

Her eyes teared up as she described the childhood experience of holding her adored Venos in her arms as they walked through the hospital admissions hall where dozens of other infants were dying in the arms of their mothers. Seeing the sadness on Nisren's face brought reality to the statistics I had researched before our interview. *The New England Journal of Medicine,* in 1992, reported that there was strong evidence that the Gulf War and trade sanctions caused a threefold increase in mortality among Iraqi children under five years of age. It was estimated that more than 46,900 children died between January and August 1991. I had always been aware of the news reports of the UN or the US placing sanctions on countries, but I had never before put an individual human face on the impact of those restrictions.

After dabbing her eyes with a tissue, Nisren continued. "I always felt so sad about Venos. I didn't want her to suffer. When she was supposed to eat, and we didn't have anything, I cried. Sometimes I didn't eat my food but saved it for her the next day. I remember taking her up to the roof when the electricity would go off and staying with her there in the moonlight until the power came back on. She was my baby to bathe, diaper, and love."

Nisren sighed as she thought about "her baby." As an aside to me, she said, "Even today Venos has problems with anemia and with her eyesight."

Caring for Venos gave Nisren real purpose in a year when she had to change from a fifth-grader focused on studying to an adult put in charge of an infant's life. It was about this time she asked her mother to teach her how to pray. She had learned something about prayer at school, and the uncle who lived with them had many religious books that she read.

"Usually kids start to say prayers at about nine years old, but Mama never suggested I pray because she always gave us choices. She was so happy when I showed interest in praying. She taught me about washing before prayers and gave me a prayer dress. Enas wanted to learn, too, so we practiced by standing beside or next to Mama. At first, I didn't pray every day, but I really liked Fridays, our holy day, when we had to really clean the house, and then had the best food we could find with all the family together. We prayed together and then ate together." Not only did this religious experience add to the unity of the family, but it also gave Nisren the strength to face the trials in her future.

Learning about prayer replaced going to school that year, but she returned to school the next year when she was in the same grade as her sister Enas and continued for one additional year. Unfortunately, completing eighth grade had to be the end of her formal education.

"I wanted to go into high school, but my dad and Munir didn't want me to travel across the city where the school was. They knew about other young girls who had been taken by Uday," she says. Known as the most hated man in Iraq, Uday Hussein, who was Saddam's first-born son, was a sadist with a taste for cruelty so strong that even Saddam recognized that he would not be a suitable heir to the presidency. Uday had a penchant for fast cars and loud, drunken parties, expensive suits and flowing robes, as well as murder, rape, and torture. He cruised the streets and ordered any girl or woman who caught his eye to be brought to his private palace, where, it was purported, he assaulted them.

It was difficult for Nisren to understand the fear that prompted her elders' decision to stop her education. "I cried and cried because I loved school."

As an adult she appreciated the protection her parents gave her but regretted not completing her high school education. When she was studying English during the first year in Colorado, she was contemplating completing a general equivalency degree (GED) but found that caring for the children occupied most of her time, and they came first.

CHAPTER 3

"He's the One I Want"

THE PHONE CALL CAME WHILE 17-YEAR-OLD NISREN WAS VISITING HER AUNT WARDA.

"You need to come home right away. You have visitors with a marriage proposal," her mother said. "The Kurdi family is here and wants to see you."

Nisren wasn't pleased. In fact, she was angry.. She was having a good time with her favorite aunt. Her father had said she could stay there all week. And besides that, she didn't want to get married. She had already had a proposal from a young man on her mother's side of the family, but she didn't like him and refused to accept the offer. In the meantime, her younger sister Enas had become engaged, which put pressure on Nisren because, according to Iraqi custom, the eldest daughter should be married first.

Her anger turned into frustrated tears. Her mother could hear her sniffling over the phone. "Just agree to see the boy," she said. A mumbled "Okay" was barely audible.

At the time of Nisren's proposal, arranged marriages were common. In Islam, marriage is traditionally considered a contract between two families, as the families' needs are considered most important. For the most part, partners come from the same kinship and religious group, in this case, Kurdish Shiite Muslim. In Iraq, nearly half of marriages were between first or second cousins. Although cousin marriages are shocking to Americans, they were once the norm throughout the world. The legal age of marriage in Iraq was 18 for both boys and girls, but a girl could marry at fifteen with parental consent. However, with the increase in financial hardship, the number of child brides had also increased because families could not afford to support their children. According to the Iraqi government in 1997, fifteen percent of marriages involved women under 18. This number jumped to more than twenty percent in 2012, with almost five percent married by the age of 15. The divorce rate in these arranged marriages was only two percent.

A second visit was arranged. The prospective groom, Raad, was in charge. He had been told that Nisren was "a beautiful girl." She had long black hair, slightly wavy, a light-skinned complexion with a smile that compelled you to talk to her, and brown eyes with flecks of green under thick, black eyelashes. Tall, athletic Raad led the procession into Nisren's house with an entourage of relatives: his sister and her baby, his mother, and a nephew, who were all seated in the front room, which served as a parlor. One of Nisren's sisters served them tea. Raad's identical twin brother, Saad, was not in the group. "That would have been confusing," Nisren laughed.

Nisren and her mother were in the bedroom. A neighbor had told Nisren Raad was a garage mechanic, which in her mind meant greasy hands, overalls, and rough manners. This description did not meet her dream of a clean-cut, handsome man who was intelligent and kind.

After the visitors were welcomed and made comfortable, a brief conversation recalled their shared lineage: Raad's paternal grandmother was the sister of Nisren's paternal grandmother. These connections would affirm the strong family bonds that are both a Kurdish and a Muslim tradition. Raad ended the pleasantries with a request.

"May I talk to Nisren?" he asked her father.

Her father agreed and called Nisren and her mother into the room. Nisren walked close behind her mom and took a seat in back of her mother's chair, partially hiding her from Raad's view but giving her a clear look at her suitor. The first thing she did was to peek around her mother's shoulder at his hands. They were clean with nicely rounded nails, albeit a bit sticky from the candy he was holding for his sister's baby. He excused himself to wash his hands, and Nisren had a full view of the man. He was imposing: six-foot two or three, broad muscular shoulders, a strong chin below an easy, somewhat mischievous, smile, and clean shaven except for a neatly trimmed mustache.

She soaked in every detail and thought to herself, "He's so handsome. I want him to be my husband."

When he strode back into the room, he sat just a few feet from her. She put her right hand over her mouth, looked down, and blushed. She had never looked that directly at a man who was not a relative. Quick thoughts of a wedding night flitted through her mind.

"Do you pray?" he asked.

The nod of her head was accompanied by a whispered "Yes."

"Is there a chance that you would wear hijab if you married me?"

Nisren didn't answer immediately. She knew that her mom had not put on the hijab until she was 29 or 30 years old, but since she had started to pray, she had been thinking about wearing the head scarf. She sneaked another peak at her prospective husband, took a breath, and said "Yes, I will."

Raad lowered his head and opened his hands. "Thanks be to God, *il hamdu Lillah*."

Without a pause for formalities and small talk, Raad looked directly at Nisren. "Can we get married soon?"

Words tumbled out of her mouth. "My sister needs to get married first, so could we wait until her wedding is finished?"

Raad smiled as he listened to the first full sentence he had heard from his prospective bride. He responded by agreeing to wait. It was better anyway because he had a romantic plan. He later told her, "We won't have a wedding until you fall in love with me." He wanted to spend time with her every weekend during the six months before their actual wedding night, so they could get to know each other. Nisren's father had told him, "You cannot sit together to talk or go outside together until you are husband and wife."

In Iraqi culture, becoming husband and wife is a legal and religious betrothal, or engagement, with the wedding and emotional and physical intimacy taking place later. Most Kurdish marriages are monogamous. However, Islam allows polygynous marriages, a man taking more than one wife. In fact, a man may have as many as four wives at one time providing that he fulfils his obligations as prescribed in Islam. Raad and Nisren's official union happened soon after their first meeting. The first step was a visit to a hospital for blood tests and then a week later, a trip to the court house to complete the paperwork regarding legal obligations and a divorce agreement, similar to a pre-nuptial in America. Since Kurdish families could not own a car, the final step was taking a taxi to visit an imam, the leader of their Muslim community, to participate in a brief religious ceremony in his office. It was necessary for a woman to wear a head covering when visiting an imam, so Raad had presented Nisren with the gift of a white dress and her first hijab, which she wore for the ceremony. Both fathers and Nisren's sisters accompanied them. It was not the custom for the mother to be present at the legal engagement. At the conclusion of the ceremony, Raad slipped a gold ring on Nisren's right hand. Then the imam put the couples' hands together and blessed them. The final step was a handshake between the fathers to confirm the union of the two families. Raad was so elated that he asked for extra copies of the official documents.

In our mid-morning living room interviews, Nisren was always dressed in her best hijab and abaya to welcome me. This day she was particularly animated, just bubbling over with details about her marriage and the handsome man who suddenly became her betrothed. This chapter in her life was like the curtain going up on a stage production with the spotlight on Nisren. The deprivations and difficulties of her family life in a city ripped apart by serial wars were replaced with the joy and excitement of falling in love. Her wide smile and giggles lit up the living room. Her delight was contagious but coupled with puzzlement on my part. How could such a momentous decision happen so quickly? It took my husband and me four years of courtship before we finally decided to tie the knot. It took Raad and Nisren about 45 minutes. I soon learned that in an arranged marriage, the stage is already set for quick acceptance of a prospective groom's proposal. Although arranged marriages do not leave much time for careful thinking or comparisons, the instructions on how to link the laces into a tight bond are very precise and governed by centuries of religious and cultural tradition. The families had already checked out the prospective couple's backgrounds and approved them. They were acceptable mates: Kurdish Shiite and second cousins from respected families. Nisren was almost 18, the legal age for a woman to marry, and most important to her, Raad was a "catch" compared to her first suitor. Then, too, expectations are different in arranged marriages. In general, love is thought to come after the marriage. This is very different from our "love comes first" tradition in Western countries. Also, our dating process or living together before marriage provides lots of time and opportunity to judge potential partners critically and deliberately. It seemed to me that our process of vetting marriage partners would produce longer lasting unions, but contrary to belief, arranged marriages win the Oscar for success. In a 2012 study by Statistic Brain, the global divorce rate for arranged marriages was six percent compared to the fifty-five percent of divorces that result from free-choice unions.

Nisren told me their courtship began soon after the ceremony at the mosque, but the wedding, which actually means the first night spent together, had to wait. A small party in the garden outside Raad's family house followed their official engagement. It wasn't easy to have any kind of celebration during these times of bombing raids in Baghdad by the US and Great Britain. In fact, just a few weeks before the party, Nisren and her family had fled to a basement shelter nearby when they heard bombs and could actually see the flames of burning buildings. In order to have a celebration that matched his enthusiasm, Raad was faced with applying for a permit to have a party at night that would, of course, require lights, but electricity was available for just a few hours in the evening. This didn't stop him. Getting around barriers was part of his skill set. Pastries were hard to come by with the current restrictions on sugar, but he managed to find a bakery that would sell him a tray of sweets. He took the goodies to the electric company to help convince the workers there to turn on the lights in his neighborhood for two more hours, so the party could light up the night. The sweet bribe worked, and the engagement was celebrated in style.

Love blossomed during the six months before the wedding night. Raad and Nisren talked about their likes and dislikes, their dreams, and their past experiences. She was surprised that her father allowed them the privacy of being alone in a room together. Her sister Enas, married just a few months before, shared a totally different experience during her engagement. She did not get to know her husband because he came to visit her only twice a month for a few minutes. She was not shy like Nisren. In fact, she wore short dresses, make-up, and her long hair styled fashionably, with the hope that a romantic connection would be in place before the actual wedding night. This did not happen. In fact, as she told her sister, "I hated him after the first night." This revelation made Nisren afraid of what would happen on that night, but the fear was balanced with Raad's sweetness and caring. No one in the family had ever talked to her about sex and what it involved. Her mother's advice was to "listen to your husband. Don't make him mad. Every girl has to do this. It's OK."

The day of the actual wedding celebration focused on the beauty of the bride: make-up applied at home, hair dressing at a salon, and a visit to a photo studio for a glamorous wedding photo that would become the only visual reminder of that special day.

"I wore two different dresses," she told me. "One was a white dress like you wear here. It was rented for the day, and the other was a traditional Kurdish dress." She stood up and hurried into the bedroom. "Let me show you. I have my wedding photo." She carefully laid the portrait on the coffee table. It was a color photo of a glamorous bride wearing bright red lipstick, eye shadow, and all the other cosmetics that brought out her beauty on this special day. She was wearing a lacy white Western style dress, and her black hair was styled in loose curls that cascaded to her shoulders, the first time I had seen her hair since we met. This well-worn photo was important enough to include in their limited belongings before they traveled to the United States.

Hussein peered down at the photo. "Who's that?"

"It's me!" Nisren responded. "Your mama."

Because Raad's family was more religiously conservative than Nisren's, the pre-wedding parties were segregated: the male relatives in Raad's house and the women in Nisren's. Her side of the family would have allowed women and boys to celebrate together in a rented wedding hall, but Raad wanted to separate the two sexes because he felt it would not be proper for the men to see Nisren before the wedding. The night before the wedding, the women in the two families, their friends, and their neighbors had a big dinner at Nisren's home with a band playing for traditional Kurdish dancing. The highlight of the party was the application of henna to the bride's hands and feet, artistically done by her mother and sister. The bride-to-be did not dance and was cautioned to show her shyness and even not to smile too much or she would appear to be too experienced or "un-virgin like." And just as in American tradition, the groom was not supposed to see the bride before the wedding, but unconventional Raad finished the men's party and appeared at Nisren's house to sit with her until 2 a.m., happy but exhausted from all the preparations he had made for his own party. She felt comfortable with Raad and assured of his kindness and gentleness, but she was still a bit nervous about the next night and the actual "wedding."

In spite of the difficult economic times, Raad decided that they should rent a hotel room for their first night together. In better times, a married couple might have had a week-long honeymoon after the wedding, but not in 1999 when economic sanctions continued to strangle the Iraqis because of Saddam's refusal to cooperate with UN weapons inspectors.

A moment of recognition struck her when she prepared to leave her family to go the hotel. "For almost 18 years, I had spent each day with my mom and dad and my brothers and sisters," she said. As she got ready to go to the taxi that would take her to the hotel, her two-year-old sister Venos, whom she had cared for since birth, was tugging on the skirt of her dress. With tears smudging her newly-mascaraed eyes, Nisren scooped her up in her arms and gave her a kiss. "Oh, sweetheart, I'm going to miss you so much."

Saying goodbye to the baby of the family was closing the door on her childhood and opening the door to life as a married woman living with her new husband in his family home. Would this be an easy transition for an eighteen-year-old? This question was pushed to the back of her mind as she excitedly looked forward to her wedding night.

In the backseat of the taxi on the way to the hotel, Nisren was protected from prying eyes with a white robe that covered her completely. Raad's sisters accompanied her in the taxi. In Kurdish tradition, the mother of the bride could not be with her daughter on this auspicious journey. In fact, she would not see her family for seven days.

After arriving at the hotel, her brother, Munir, said a blessing on the couple and Raad transferred her engagement ring to her left hand. Someone in the wedding party suggested that they have dinner in the hotel dining room. Raad was quick to say, "I don't want dinner. I just want to get married." As the couple walked toward the elevator that would take them to their room, Nisren's brother suggested, "If you want, call me back when you're done." He was not referring to dinner.

It is a custom, before consummating a marriage, for the couple to clip a small piece of white cloth to the bed sheet to catch the drops of blood that would prove the bride was a virgin. That piece of cloth would later be placed in a bag to be shown to the groom's parents before it was taken to the bride's house. Tradition says that a bride has to tell her husband if she is not a virgin and why. If an accident may have damaged her virginity, a police report would have to be made to verify this condition. If the bride and groom have had sexual relations prior to the wedding, they might cut a finger to produce the specimen of blood to preserve the family's honor. If it is discovered on the wedding night that she is not a virgin and has had relations with another man, she promptly will be divorced and returned to her family. To protect the family honor, her father, a brother, or another male relative could legally take her life in an "honor killing." What underlies this centuries-old practice is the cultural belief that women's bodies are the site of honor and that their sexuality must be controlled in order to avoid bringing dishonor upon the entire family. In spite of the fact that Iraqi women have enjoyed more freedoms than women in many other countries in the Middle East, honor killings still prevail as the result of conservative tribal norms. Such cases can be difficult to document. An Iraqi Human Rights Ministry report said 249 Iraqi women were murdered in 2010, including those killed for "honor crimes," without giving a breakdown.

After their wedding night, Nisren's belief that her new husband was "sweet and gentle" was confirmed. Raad pronounced his satisfaction by proclaiming, "I'm hungry for dinner now." Nisren joined Raad's household the next day. He was the only married son living there, in addition to seven unmarried brothers. Two sisters were already married and living with their husbands in their houses.

I pondered how lucky this couple was to find love in an arranged marriage that seemed to have become even stronger in a new country that gives women a stronger role. Nisren jokingly said, "Raad was teasing me after we came here. He said he could have one wife in Iraq and one here in the States. I told him I could put him in jail because I have more power here."

Raad's house was large with a garden, parking space, a big kitchen, five bedrooms, and a large salon. If they chose to, each son who married could live in the house in a bedroom upstairs. Nisren quickly carved out a role for herself. She would do the tasks she loved to do the most: sweeping, mopping, cleaning windows, and washing clothes by hand. She had watched her mother do these jobs to perfection, and she followed in her footsteps. Raad's mom had two daughters and eight sons, including Raad's twin brother, Saad. She was in her 60s, so she welcomed her new daughter-in-law with open arms. She did the shopping, and Nisren did all the housework, much to Nisren's satisfaction. Cooking meals was only an occasional task.

"I had never cooked much," Nisren said, "so when I needed to know how to prepare a dish, I quietly called my sister or mom, so nobody else knew. One time I told Raad that I didn't really know how to cook. He laughed and said, 'If I'd known that, I wouldn't have married you.'"

Nisren loved her new family, and they loved her. Raad's twin brother, Saad, was very kind to her. He had become engaged on the same day as Raad, but unfortunately, his wife had divorced him before the actual wedding night. He was planning to marry again. The brothers were very close, spending almost every hour of the day together in college classes, working with cars, and practicing tae kwon do at a local club. "It was strange." Nisren said. "If Raad hurt his finger at work, then later that day the same thing would happen to Saad." However, the brothers were quite different in temperament. Saad, who was a little shorter and not quite as muscular, easily talked about his feelings and was more emotional. Raad was always the strong man who never showed any weakness.

Much to Nisren's disappointment, it didn't take long before the newly-wed stage was over. She didn't resent this turning point but accepted it as part of a typical marriage. "Raad and I didn't have much time together," she said. After Raad came home from work, he would sit down with the extended family for dinner and then leave the house to socialize with his brothers and friends until midnight. Because there were more sons who could earn money, Raad's life was very different from life in Nisren's household. As a young man, Raad had worked, gone to school, practiced tae kwon do in the gym, played soccer with friends, and basically spent the whole day outside the house. This pattern, other than school, continued after marriage, but a new milestone was added to their lives.

Nisren became pregnant early in their marriage. The impending joy of a baby was clouded by worry about the need for a Caesarean section, the cost of hospital care (which had previously been free in government hospitals), and rumors about the declining quality of that care. The infrastructure in Baghdad was crumbling. Hunger and deprivation persisted, and the doomsday of September 11, 2001, and the US invasion into Iraq was coming closer. In March 2000, a year after their marriage, Nisren and Raad had a daughter, Noor, meaning "the light" in Arabic.

"I went into labor before the surgery, but the nurses wouldn't give me any pain pills. All they could offer were shouts of 'Push!' Anesthesia was reserved for the necessary Caesarean section. "When I woke up, all I could remember was the yelling of the nurses."

In spite of the British and American air strikes in Iraq and the lack of food and medicine, Noor truly became the bright spot in their daily lives. Although they weren't planning to have another baby until the situation in Baghdad had improved, Nisren got pregnant again. The auto repair business had provided very little money over the previous three years because of the suffering economy. It was too expensive to visit a doctor for pre-natal care. When Nisren was in her ninth month, she could no longer feel the baby moving. She confided in Raad's sister, who told her she had to go to the hospital immediately. The doctor at the hospital diagnosed her with gestational diabetes and surmised that the baby was "so tired," it wasn't moving normally. Nisren had a C-section the next day and delivered a four-kilo (8.8 pound) baby boy, whom they named Mohammed. During her only night in the hospital, Raad called her and cautioned, "Don't leave the baby alone for even a minute. He might be kidnapped and sold." There were rumors that babies, especially boys, were being stolen and sold for adoption, and some babies were even being sold for organ donations.

In the government hospital, patients paid for every service rendered: the nurse who brings the baby to the mother, each medical professional involved in the birth, and even the cleaner and the tea-server. Raad and Nisren found that they were short of money when they were told the cost of taking the baby home the next day. "If you don't give us the money now, we don't give you the baby" was the official policy. Raad quickly called on family members for extra funds, so they could take Mohammed home. After leaving the hospital, Nisren went to her mother's crowded apartment for a week and then home to Raad's house, which provided more comfort and space for the mother and new baby. Her mother came with her to assist her for two more weeks.

Protecting their two children and providing for food and housing became central to their lives.

CHAPTER 4

Invasion and Opportunity

WHEN HIJACKED AIRPLANES OBLITERATED THE WORLD TRADE CENTER'S
TWIN TOWERS AND THE PENTAGON ON SEPTEMBER 11, 2001, IRAQ BECAME
PART OF US PRESIDENT GEORGE W. BUSH'S "AXIS OF EVIL." Despite this,
the incident barely registered among Baghdad citizens. After suffering
carnage at home for twenty years, another bombing a world away was
unremarkable. By then, most Iraqis had seen such violence and misery
first hand. Although it was a highly-militarized country, Iraq was
hardly a nation of well-equipped warriors. In fact, many Iraqi soldiers
wore only their street clothes and flip-flops. Saddam responded to
President Bush's accusations with the same charge of "Evil" when the
US initiated the invasion of Iraq on March 20, 2003. The US, along
with coalition forces, primarily from the United Kingdom, started the
conflict just ninety minutes after the US-imposed deadline passed for
Saddam to leave Iraq or face war. President Bush and his advisors
built much of their case for war on the idea that Iraq possessed or
was in the process of building weapons of mass destruction and was
deceiving UN weapons inspectors. President Bush announced in a
television address, "At this hour, American and coalition forces are
in the early stages of military operations to disarm Iraq, to free its
people, and to defend the world from grave danger. . . ."

Also at that hour, Nisren, Raad, one-year-old Mohammed, and two-year-old Noor could hear government buildings and military installations being bombed by Tomahawk cruise missiles from US fighter bombers and warships stationed in the Persian Gulf. Luckily, their area of Baghdad remained safe, but they didn't know what would happen when American troops actually entered the city. It was assumed that there would be fighting in Baghdad, so Nisren and the children went to the countryside thirty miles away to stay with her mother's relatives. Many of their neighbors and other families also had left Baghdad to go outside the city where they could stay in empty school buildings or in the homes of extended family members. They expected American troops to successfully occupy Baghdad but were worried about how much collateral damage would be done to the city in the fight with Saddam's army.

Raad and some of his brothers were trapped at home where they clustered around the radio trying to find out what was happening. "Saddam was smart. He had put all his military power, Ba'ath party guards, security, and police, in the streets. If we put our heads outside the front door, somebody would question us," Raad said. On the radio, they heard the Americans were coming from the airport into Baghdad city. They waited in the dark listening to the sound of explosions coming closer and closer to them. Then suddenly it stopped. "We put our heads out and saw big tanks rolling down the streets."

Saddam loyalists had quickly changed their regime uniforms, left their guns behind, and fled for their lives. As morning started to dawn, everyone came out on the streets and walked toward a huge concrete slab under a demolished warehouse that had been transformed into an Iraqi military bunker. As they walked, a scattered group of neighbors morphed into thousands of Iraqis, smiling and shouting. The mantra of "We love Saddam" had become "We love Americans."

Raad and his brothers joined the group. When they got to the bunker, they saw Humvees, tanks, and special forces of US Marines digging under the concrete. American intelligence had told them of the possibility that Saddam had kept members of the Kuwaiti royal family as hostages for twelve years. The Marines were searching for them. It was customary for secret prisons to be built under hospitals and other government buildings. The noise of the crowd obliterated the voice of a Marine commander who was shouting in English, "Shut up! Be quiet!" as the Marines tried to use listening devices detect any voices under the concrete. Raad was near the front of the crowd.

The commander pointed at him, "You! Come here! Do you speak English?"

Raad paused a moment, mentally translating the English before he yelled back. Although he had studied some English in high school and watched numerous American videos, the only time he spoke the language was when he was working out in the tae kwon do gym where the South Korean owners used English.

"I speak a little," Raad shouted back, while he stepped forward and up on the concrete slab.

"What's your name?" the commander asked.

"My name's Raad."

"Okay, Rashid. Here's a microphone. Get up there, and tell the people to be quiet and to go back to their houses."

In a voice that could halt the flow of the Tigris and Euphrates rivers, Raad commanded the crowd to be quiet and to move back, so the Marines could use their listening devices. He repeated the order several times before the people focused their attention on the man speaking Arabic to them in a loud, deep voice. In a few minutes, there was silence as the crowd backed away from the warehouse. As the bystanders receded, two officers approached Raad.

"You're Rashid, right?"

"No, my name's Raad."

"Okay, Rashid. Can you come back tomorrow to help us?"

He laughed and gave up on correcting them. "I'll be here."

On his way to the command post bunker the next day, he had a call for help from a friend whose cousin was hit by a crystal bomb, a graphite explosive used to disable electrical systems. The friend asked if Raad could get a vehicle to take the bleeding man to an American post for medical help. He got a truck and found a medic to treat the wounds. The medics were relieved to have an English-speaker with them, and Raad was eager to hear what they knew about the invasion. He stayed with the group for the remainder of the day and returned at their request the next day. This chance meeting with Marine medics turned into more requests for his interpretation and his knowledge of Baghdad, the people, and the culture.

"We need people like you. Why don't you come help us at one of our posts every day?" one of the Marines said. "We'll pay you."

"I'm not doing this for money, just to help you guys," he said. They gave him a location where he could register as an interpreter. Raad thought about the offer for a few days. Since there had been no work for him at the auto shop for more than a month, he decided to visit the suggested post. He was wearing the same t-shirt he had worn on the day he was called on to speak over the microphone. The same officer who called on him recognized him as "Rashid" and offered him a job. They gave him an official badge to wear but no uniform, body armor, or other protection.

Each day he worked with one of the colonels on a specific mission from 6 a.m. to 4 or 5 p.m. and then went home to his family. "It was like a normal job. No secrecy. No risk," he said. "My neighbors knew that I was working with the Americans, and that was okay."

Raad had many talents to offer the Marines: an outgoing, strong personality backed up by intelligence, the ability to smooth over communication between local tribal and sectarian groups and the

US military, and his knowledge of the more than 85 neighborhoods that comprised Baghdad city. He helped the military to rout out Ba'ath party members by informing them of possible locations where they were hiding. He and other "Terps," as they were called, also dealt with the Army's infrastructure improvement: sewer, roads, buildings, councils, plus the new Iraqi army and security forces. "I would go to other units, throughout the neighborhoods, and to hospitals in the midst of Humvees, tanks, and Marines. I was feeling free and happy," Raad remembered. Even though officers and troops received cultural training before being sent to Iraq, Raad discovered that they had very little practical knowledge. In conversation one day, Raad used the thumbs up gesture to signal that everything was okay. "How come you're doing that?" an officer challenged. "We were taught it meant 'Fuck you.'" Evidently their instructor had mixed up the fingers.

At the end of each day, the officer in charge would pull ten dollars from his pocket and force him to take it. "The money would only buy a pair of pants," Raad said. "My real pay was the excitement I felt about helping the Americans and my country."

During the first few weeks of his job, Baghdad was bombed on a daily basis, destroying many government buildings. Seeing statues of Saddam toppled re-enforced the citizens' feelings of freedom from a repressive regime that had imprisoned and killed so many. Groups of Iraqis angry with the regime looted and sometimes burned stores and homes. "Men, women, and children stole from empty houses, taking anything they could find, even doors and windows," Nisren said with disgust, adding that "these angry people felt that they deserved to take what they considered was theirs."

Coupled with the anger was optimism. Just a month after the invasion, people talked to the Americans, invited them to their homes, and a US-appointed Governing Council was set up. However, the designers of Operation Iraqi Freedom had failed to answer a vital question: "After Saddam, what next?"

This unanswered question, suggested army Colonel Joe Rice in a later interview, led to the US failure to prepare adequately for the post-war environment. Iraqis expectations of the US presence were not met when electricity, water, and other services were not restored early in the game. Looting, a sign of the ripping apart of the society, was just one result of this failure. "The people suffered physical damage but also damage to the social fabric of their lives," he said. As a former mayor of the city of Glendale, Colorado, Rice had local government experience that led him to be appointed to the Baghdad Council's Working Group. He initiated a caucus process that encouraged people in the neighborhoods to meet together to form their own local council, which, in turn, would choose a representative to the district group, and then appoint a representative to the city council. "This is a time-honored democratic method," Rice commented. "We tried hard not to shake the established system but to let the people figure it out for themselves. We often interfered just enough to prevent bad situations from developing but not enough to help institutions to develop." Unfortunately, according to Rice, the US left in the middle ground. "We would pull back from Iraq with security and personnel and then get back in, and pull back again instead of keeping institutions and relationships going."

From Raad's point of view in the first few weeks after the invasion, "Good things were happening so fast. Saddam was caught, and his sons were killed. People were excited and hopeful. It was like being in a noisy, crazy disco where you get a headache and have to go outside to breathe." Recognition that the interpreters were a critical link between the US military and the Iraqi populace produced a big change in Raad's position several months later. He became an official employee. Titan, a San Diego translation company originally known as Titan Communications Corporation, received the Department of Defense contract to hire local Iraqi interpreters. "We had to pass a test, sign a contract, wear an official badge, and receive a monthly salary of about 450 dollars, which was double what I had made as an auto mechanic the year before the invasion," Raad explained. It was also possible for interpreters to sign up to be evacuated if necessary. "At this time, evacuation didn't seem like a possibility, and I didn't want to go back to my usual life, so I put my name on the list."

"In one night everything changed," Raad said. "The morning of April 15, 2003 I followed my usual routine and took a taxi to the base I was assigned to. The driver was in a hurry to get me out of the car. I walked toward the base where people are usually standing and talking. Instead, a group of security officers stopped me. Luckily, one of them recognized me. He was surprised that I had gotten safely to the base."

When Raad asked them what was going on, they told him the Shia militias loyal to radical cleric, Muqtada al-Sadr, had attacked coalition forces. "In that one night from my base we had ten "cowboys" [interpreters] hit, 73 soldiers wounded, and three or four killed. When I went to my colonel's office, I saw my guys dirty and scared."

The colonel asked him for advice. Raad suggested getting the tribal and religious sheiks, or leaders, together in a meeting to see what was behind the attack. He arranged the meeting, which lasted several hours. Ideas were exchanged but no decisions reached. When Raad returned from the meeting, he saw his brother and brother-in-law waiting for him.

"Do you know what happened at home?" his brother asked. "Didn't you look behind you when you left the house this morning?"

What Raad had not seen was the black, spray-painted word "Traitor" on the front of his house. When he heard this news, shock and anger sent him immediately to his colonel, who handed him a pistol to use as protection for him and his family.

"When we got home, we washed away the sign, and I got my family out of the house to stay with relatives. I decided I had to quit my job. Now they knew where I lived." For a month, he made it a point to sit in front of his house, so everyone would see that he had quit working with the Americans. A month later, he decided to go back, and his twin brother, who had recently signed on, accompanied him but was assigned to a different unit. Then he learned other interpreters who had not quit their jobs had been killed. Why did he return to a job that endangered both him and his family? "I liked what I was doing, and I was good at it. I was part of an American group that I respected. I was making a difference."

Soon after Raad's return to work, more American troops arrived, and more Iraqi men and women were needed as interpreters. Titan hired more than 8,000 interpreters who, on average, received $12,000 a year, according to an *Pro Publica* report, to do what the Associated Press called "one of the most dangerous civilian jobs in one of the most dangerous countries: translating Arabic for the US military in Iraq." The same report estimated there were over 1200 local interpreters severely injured and 360 interpreters killed between the beginning of the war and the so-called surge in 2007 when Iraqi interpreters were hired on an even wider basis. Because interpreters were usually seen standing between the commander and another Iraqi, they became easy targets for insurgents gunfire.

Drastic changes were in store for Raad and his family. He was finally issued the protective equipment he needed: a camouflage uniform, a Kevlar helmet and vest, body armor, and ear-and-eye protection, the same items given to US troops and foreign contractors. He also was given a weapon to carry home but not to take on missions. Even his name was changed to prevent recognition by Iraqis. Because

Raad and Saad were twins, they officially became Tom and Jerry. Other Terps were denoted as Muchacho, James, John, and so on. In this stage of the game, the duties of interpreters were expanded to include more than translation; they were cultural advisors, policy analysts, and intelligence officers. They provided a grounds-eye view of situations and a link between the US military and civilians. Raad accompanied officers in the Marines and later in the US Army to meetings with local Iraqi leaders, to tribal funerals to ease the tension when US personnel were involved in the death, and in the search for Saddam Hussein's hiding place. He was proud to assume the tasks required, while at the same time, he was well aware of the dangers involved with supporting what some Iraqi factions called the enemy.

In many Iraqis' minds, appreciation of the American military changed soon after the invasion. Chaos was unleashed as Baghdad became a major center for resistance against the American occupiers. In December, nine months after the invasion ended, Saddam surrendered to US troops when he was found hiding near Tikrit. At the same time, major figures from the Ba'ath regime were tracked down and arrested. The Ba'ath Party was decimated, and an entity known as the Coalition Provisional Authority (CPA), headed by a senior American diplomat, assumed the governance of Iraq. As many as 85,000 Ba'ath Party members lost their jobs as a result of a CPA order. This action fueled the fire of opposition to the American-led war. As collaborators with the CPA, interpreters were targeted with death threats, kidnappings, or violent and sometimes deadly attacks by groups such as the Mahdi Army or Al-Qaeda in Iraq. Radical Shiite cleric Muqtada al-Sadr gained a following of people who now looked at the occupying forces as enemies. Saddam had killed al-Sadr's father and brothers, so he had fled to Iran and then returned. He was opposed to the coalition-appointed Iraqi Governing Council, and in a television interview with reporter Bob Simon of *60 Minutes*, he famously said "Saddam was the little serpent, but America is the big serpent." Rumors began painting the Terps as traitors, saying they were feeding Americans false information, stealing houses, raping women, and abusing prisoners.

"People began asking me 'Why did you bring the Americans here?' I couldn't believe they thought that I, just a simple person, could bring all these soldiers, all these tanks here. I'm just a normal man trying to help my country," Raad said. Many Iraqis soon began to believe the stories, especially as the promised benefits of the American occupation failed to materialize. Extermination of interpreters was a way to express their disappointment and revenge.

Fear was always an unwanted guest in the many places Nisren had lived as a child. Its impact doubled when Raad became an official interpreter. "Eyes were watching the interpreters and their families," she said. "They were just waiting to report any activity related to the Americans to local Mahdi Army spies. We moved at least five times because neighbors started noticing when Raad came and went."

He frequently had to stay on the military base because travel to his family posed a threat. In fact, commuting from home to work was as dangerous as on-the-job missions. Nisren remembered Mohammed's first birthday without his father at home: "I wanted to have a party for Mohammed, but I couldn't be seen going outside to buy a cake or juice, so we ate dates with a candle on one and drank milk. I felt like I was in jail, but I guess we were lucky to just have a place to live."

Without stopping for breath, her words race toward the finish line of this episode in her life. "It was a scary and dangerous time. If the neighbors found out that Raad was an interpreter, we would have to move again. I told lies to the kids about what their dad was doing. For six years, I couldn't sleep at night. In the morning after I got

Mohammed and Noor to school, I would call the bus driver to see if the kids had gotten there safely. Then I might take a nap." Through their father's persuasive tactics, Mohammed and Noor were enrolled in a top-ranking Catholic primary school. Before Raad made a special visit to the school, they would only accept girls. "I tried many ways to get Mohammed accepted, but the Sisters objected to allowing boys to study there." One day, carrying the official laptop he used in his work, he made a visit to the headmistress. When he saw she was occupied with other people, he asked her to speak in private with him. "I told her to get those people out and to sit down so we could talk. I opened the lap top to show her I was an official interpreter with the US Army. Then I told her just to call on me if she needed extra security for the school or anything else." The next day Mohammed was admitted to the school.

Transportation was important for interpreters in order for them to quickly move around the city as needed. Raad used a motorcycle, so he could maneuver the narrow Baghdad streets at high speeds and with less visibility. His brother chose to drive a car to accomplish his duties. The twins were different in their attitudes toward danger. Raad was cautious and aware of his surroundings. Saad was more naïve and didn't think anyone was watching him. He didn't listen to his brother who frequently warned him to be alert and always look behind him. "You can't relax for even a minute," Raad advised him.

In his third year of work, Raad was in a meeting with US Army officers when he started to feel sick to his stomach. He left the meeting to go to the bathroom.

"I felt something was wrong. Something had happened," he told Nisren. What he didn't know until several hours later was that his brother had been killed at the exact time that he had felt ill and left the meeting. Nisren tells me that Saad, driving on a main street, had been followed by al-Sadr's men in two cars. They planned to kidnap him to get information about US actions in the area. Saad saw the cars behind him and sped up to get away from them. He couldn't maneuver around a concrete barrier, so he hit it head on and rolled the car. When his pursuers saw the accident, they changed their minds about kidnapping. Instead, they wanted to be sure he was dead. As Saad tried to get out of the car, he was shot. When Raad and Nisren saw photos of the accident, they saw that the car was riddled with bullets. The government performed an autopsy on the body to determine how Saad died. "Multiple gunshot wounds" was listed as the cause of death.

Raad didn't sleep for a week after Saad's death. "It was the first time I had seen him cry," Nisren says. "Saad was also like a brother to me. He stayed with me in the hospital when Noor was born and brought me ice cream as a treat. His wife had children at almost the same times as I had Noor and Mohammed."

After Saad's death, Nisren and her father begged Raad to stop working with the US Army. He quit for two months and then went out again. Nisren said, "I cried so much about the danger he faced every day."

In December 2006, three years after the US invasion and Raad's decision to be an interpreter, Saddam Hussein was judged by an Iraqi Criminal Justice Tribunal and found guilty for crimes against humanity. He was hanged. In 2007, thousands more US troops were dispatched to shore up security in Baghdad. Considered the deadliest year of the invasion, 2007 statistics recorded 26,000 civilian deaths and 904 US soldiers killed in violence, according to *Statista: The Statistics Portal*. At the same time, the National Defense Authorization Act authorized the issuance of up to 50 Special Immigrant Visas (SIVs) annually to Iraqi and Afghan translators and interpreters working for the US military. The number was expanded to 500 annually for 2007 and 2008. Spouses, as well as unmarried children younger than 21 were granted SIVs and could travel with the interpreter or could follow to join him or her after they had been admitted to the United States.

Raad saw other interpreters applying for SIVs that would allow them to go to new lives in the United States with the status of legal permanent resident or "green card holder." He decided to begin the process of application before telling Nisren and the children. He finished the paperwork and requested letters of recommendation from his commanders, even receiving one from General David Petraeus, then the commanding general in Iraq. It took him six months to finally decide to activate his application.

"I hoped that things would change, and I could continue working with the US military, but it was just too dangerous for my family," he said. Taking his family thousands of miles across the world from Baghdad was the biggest decision he would ever make. However, with hopes for a better future for his family, he submitted his application for an SIV. The final step was finding a sponsor in the US who would help him to settle in a specific city, a seemingly impossible task for someone without American connections. On several of his early deployments to Iraq, US Army Colonel Joe Rice had met Raad. When he ran into him at a meeting, the Colonel expressed surprise that "Tom," as he called him, had not joined other interpreters who were getting visas to re-locate to the US.

"Why are you still here after all these years?" Rice asked him.

"I've done all the paperwork, but I don't have a sponsor yet."

"That's not a problem. I'd be happy to sponsor you," Rice offered.

He knew Raad had served well in his job as an interpreter and recognized the imminent danger that he and his family faced. He also recognized Raad's dedication to progress in Iraq, his good character, and his ability to face new situations, all traits that would aid his adjustment to life in another country. Colonel Rice was generous in his offer and subsequently served as a sponsor for several other Iraqis.

A firm handshake between the two men confirmed this momentous turning point in the family's lives.

"How would you like to take your family to Colorado?" Rice asked.

Raad had never heard of Colorado, but he was relieved and eager to go anywhere that would provide safety and hope. Because Colonel Rice was still on active duty, he told Raad he would arrange for contacts in Littleton, Colorado, to assist him when he and his family arrived.

Now Raad could tell Nisren about the prospect of going to America, but what would she think about leaving Baghdad, the only home she had ever known? Could she thrive without the support and love of her family?

CHAPTER 5

Safe at Last

SAAD'S CAR, POCK-MARKED BY BULLETS, BUBBLED TO THE SURFACE OF NISREN'S MIND EVERY TIME SHE LOOKED AT HER OWN HUSBAND, HIS IDENTICAL TWIN. Is Raad the next target? she worried. Are the children safe?

Nisren knew that other interpreters and their families had fled to the United States but did not know that Raad had applied for refugee resettlement. When he shared the news with her that he had a sponsor, it turned the page on her premonitions.

"I was dead before, but when Raad told me about the US, I felt alive again. I had been thinking only about losing my husband and something happening to the kids," Nisren told me. "I wasn't thinking how hard it would be to leave my own family behind."

The family had just a few weeks to prepare for their departure. Raad suggested that he would go first and then come back to get Nisren and the children later, but she rejected that plan. She was afraid to be without him for the four months it would take to process the visa.

When the family finally boarded the commercial jetliner for their first flight ever, they were excited but conflicted. Some other refugees on board the plane were crying as they looked out the windows at their families waving goodbye. When they got to their first stop in Jordan, Nisren used her phone to call her brother and report on their trip. Eight-year-old Noor spoke to her uncle and, in tears, told him she wanted to go back home.

"I started to think 'What have I done? When will I see my family again?'" Nisren said. "Raad had told me it might be five years before we could go back to visit." In those years, Nisren knew her parents might not even be alive because of their health issues. There was no turning back. No one knew what the future held for them.

From Baghdad to Jordan to Washington DC where they missed their flight to Denver made for a tedious 25-hour trip. Through his friend and colleague, Susan Thornton, Colonel Rice had arranged for board members of LI3, the Littleton Immigrant Integration Initiative, to assist the family when they arrived. Susan informed us of our first opportunity as a new board: Welcoming an Iraqi family and assisting them in settling into a new country, a different culture, a puzzling language, and unique surroundings. Mika, Susan, and I eagerly volunteered for the assignment. My first task was to greet them at the Denver airport and take them to the motel I had arranged. When they didn't arrive on the designated flight and couldn't be located on the airline roster, my husband and I left a message at the information desk with the name of the motel where their room was reserved. At 10 p.m., an exhausted family of four de-planed their flight, took a train to baggage claim, and received a message about the motel that had been arranged for them. Luckily, they found a taxi driver who spoke some Arabic, and Nisren, Noor, and Mohammed promptly fell asleep on the drive to the motel.

"We are finally here," Raad announced when the taxi pulled up in front of the motel. "Wake up!" They showered and slept until the sun came up the next day.

On a warm, sunny August morning five years after their arrival in Colorado, I pulled my car around the corner to the duplex. It was a perfect day for kids to be playing outdoors, but the backyard was empty of the toys and bikes that occupied other families' play spaces. The yard wasn't fenced, but Nisren would not want Hussein outdoors by himself anyway. She complained that "the minute we go outside to walk or to the park, he runs, and I can't get him to stay with me." To offset the lack of play time outdoors, the whole family spent part of each weekend in a nearby park. When Nisren welcomed me at the door, she reminded me that this month was their fifth anniversary in the United States. It seemed an appropriate time to talk about those first days. Two-year-old Hussein, who wasn't even born at that time, was bouncing up and down on the sofa, eager to have a visitor but not ready to be quiet. Nisren, always patient and never scolding, calmed him down with a glass of juice and a small box of plastic toys.

Nisren remembered every detail of their arrival and the initial weeks of amazement and adjustment. "That night in the motel was the first time I had slept through the night for six years, the first time I hadn't worried about danger to my family. In Iraq, my ears were like rabbit ears. I was always listening for someone trying to open the door." When they walked out of the motel the next morning, they were greeted by a typical Colorado day with bright sunshine, blue skies, and a clear view of the Rocky Mountains.

Nisren took a deep breath and slowly released it with a smile. "The air smelled beautiful. It was like breathing life."

The family decided to take a walk in the neighborhood around the motel with no purpose in mind other than enjoying their surroundings. "It was a wonderful day. Everything was different and beautiful. Green trees, grass. The kids loved it and wanted to keep walking until we were afraid of getting lost."

Later in the day, Mika met them at the motel and drove them around the city. An important contact in the first few days was the African Community Center (ACC), which supports resettlement of refugees who have fled persecution in countries throughout the world.

Mika accompanied them to the ACC where a case-worker explained the aid that they qualified for while they were adjusting to life in the United States and becoming self-sufficient. Unlike Raad, refugees who connected with this agency before they entered the US were met at the airport, situated in temporary housing, and scheduled for an orientation at the ACC. Then they were given a one-time cash grant of approximately $1000 for each family member with the caution that they had just 90 days to become self-sufficient. This money had to stretch far enough for apartment deposit and rental, furnishings, cooking utensils, cleaning supplies, food, and transportation. At the end of the three-month period, they must have employment and be able to pay all the bills. Raad's situation was a bit different. He was not part of this program when he left Baghdad. Although his air fare was paid for, he had to pay back the money when he was able. Since he already had contacts in Denver and the opportunity for work, he was a step ahead of most refugees. The ACC filled the gap by giving him money for apartment rental and deposit and issued him a bus pass to help with transportation for the many tasks required for a new start in a new country. The family also qualified for state and federal subsidies available to people living below the poverty line. They were issued a credit from the Denver Department of Human Services for food and a monthly allotment and officially became part of TANF (Temporary Assistance for Needy Families), which qualified them for Medicaid, and food stamps, which would be discontinued when Raad was officially employed.

"I appreciated the help ACC gave me. This, plus the connections Joe Rice made to the Littleton immigrant group, made it much easier to get settled. I wanted to become part of life in America as fast as I could." Raad said.

Raad, Nisren, Noor, and Mohammed were part of a total of 74,602 refugees admitted to the United States during 2009. Arrivals from Iraq included 18,709 refugees, as well as 1,764 SIVs, which comprised the largest admission group, according to the Office of Refugee Resettlement, US Department of Health and Human Services.

Finding a place to live was next on the to-do list. Mika introduced them to an Egyptian immigrant from her church who lived in a small apartment building in an older part of Littleton close to an elementary school and not far from where Raad had prospects for a job. The friendly Arabic-speaking gentleman introduced them to the apartment manager, who leased them a two-bedroom apartment, and introduced them to their neighbors. Mika contacted the local Optimists Club, which provided them with some used furniture

Raad needed employment within 90 days. Susan contacted the owner of a local automobile dealership, who asked the manager to interview Raad. After filling out an application and meeting the manager, he was hired on probation as an auto mechanic. Tools for his job were expensive, so the Optimists Club donated money to the Littleton Immigration Initiative, the nonprofit we had just initiated, to buy the kit of tools.

Nisren soon realized that she needed basic English language skills to help her family and needed them in a hurry, so she enrolled in an "English as a second language" (ESL) program at Littleton's Bemis Library. She fell in love with the first library she had ever been in, and she thrived in the class with a teacher who appreciated her enthusiasm to learn the language. In a small way, these classes gave her the opportunity, at twenty-six, that she had missed when she was forced to leave school at fourteen. "The teacher taught us to speak without being afraid the words were wrong," she said. "Sometimes it was funny, but that was okay. I remember saying 'Put the letter in the *ambulance* because *ambulance* and *envelope* sounded the same to me."

I couldn't resist sharing a similar experience with her when I was learning Arabic in Cairo. I had a terrible time pronouncing the word for bathroom, *ham'mam*, and not pronouncing the extra *m* sound, so it came out *hama'am*, which is the word for pigeon. Instead of asking someone 'Where is the bathroom?' I ended up asking "Where is the pigeon?" Nisren giggled with appreciation at my language gaffe.

"I knew some English words from movies and hearing others, but speaking was difficult," she confided "I learned fast because knew I would have to help the kids and go shopping for food." When she looked back on those first few weeks, she was amazed at how much was achieved thanks to Mika and Susan. In her acquaintance with other immigrants over the five years, she realized that most refugees and immigrants do not have the necessary contacts to get settled that quickly. When Raad reflected on those initial months in a later interview, he commented, "The faster you can fit into society in a new country, the better you can adjust. We were so lucky to have good people to help us."

Unfortunately, the honeymoon period of loving everything about their adopted home didn't last long. Tasks of daily living confronted the family. "At first, we didn't have a car and didn't know where to go for food. It was difficult because the store was too far away to walk to," Nisren explained. Mika took them to the King Soopers market where they picked food they knew would fit their Muslim restrictions which, in this case, meant mostly vegetables, fruit, and bread but no pork or other meats because they were not *halal*, killed and processed according to Muslim rules. To make their food adjustment even more disconcerting, a week after they arrived was the end of Ramadan. The conclusion of the 30 days of fasting from daylight to dawn was the *Eid*, or feast, when they would go to the mosque to pray and get together with the family to break the fast with special foods and sweets, conversation, and watching movies. Luckily, they were eating only one meal a day because they were fasting during daylight hours, but unluckily, they had no family in Colorado to help them celebrate the feast day.

Getting settled was difficult, but it was heightened by the fact that telephones in Iraq were not working at the very time they were desperate to talk to their relatives. Although it wasn't as good as direct communication, Raad discovered he could go to the library to use a computer to message his family. Because Nisren's family didn't have a computer, Raad's father would share their information with her family.

Noor and Mohammed had teeter-tottering emotions about their new country. The upswing was excitement about parks, malls, and playgrounds they had never seen before, but the downswing was dismay at not understanding the language and fear of going to an American school where they would not be like the other kids. Noor had completed fifth grade in Baghdad, but it was decided by the principal at East Elementary School that fourth grade would provide a better transition for her. Mohammed entered second grade at the same elementary school, which offered excellent ESL instruction. Much to the children's surprise, there were many children from different countries who were also struggling with language learning.

I was delighted when Noor, then fifteen, came down the stairs and into the living room where Nisren and I were continuing the interview about their first months in Colorado. She was at home today because it was a faculty work day at Littleton High School with no classes in session. When I greeted her, she leaned down to give me an awkward hug. She was no longer the shy little girl who wanted to go home to be with her cousins. Today she was a confident, attractive teenager wearing jeans, a long-sleeved blue shirt, and a white hijab. She sat down on the sofa next to her mom. Folding her bare feet up next to her, she listened intently as I recorded her mom's responses. Nisren finished a sentence, looked over at Noor, and nodded that it was her turn to chime in. I asked Noor what she remembered about their arrival.

"I was too young to even understand why we were leaving

Baghdad," she said with a perfect American accent. "My friends were my cousins. It hit me when we started school that I was all alone. I didn't have any friends, and I was lonely for almost a year. At school nobody picked on me, but everybody around me talked to each other, and I didn't know what was going on. There was a boy who spoke Arabic, but I couldn't understand him,"

With a defiant shake of her head, she said, "I *did* know that I didn't want to be the only one who didn't speak English. That's why I learned so fast. I wanted to be part of everything."

Nisren interrupted with a smile. "Now the teachers tell me that she talks too much."

Noor continued, "I had the nicest teachers. They cared about me, not just my learning, but my inclusion with friends, the whole person. I now have friends from elementary school time. In one year, I could understand what people were saying, but couldn't speak back much. By eighth grade, all was OK. Now I speak English, some Kurdish, and Arabic."

I recalled the photo of the family soon after they arrived. Noor, dressed like any American ten-year-old girl, looked shy and embarrassed. "You've certainly grown up since then," I said. She was taller than her mom now and slim. She had deep brown, thickly-lashed eyes that required no mascara to be striking and a creamy complexion dotted with a few adolescent blemishes.

"You weren't wearing a hijab when I first met you," I said.

She leaned forward, elbows on her knees. "I thought about it when we joined a group at the mosque, and I met other girls wearing hijab. When we Skyped with family in Iraq, I saw my girl cousins had already started wearing hijab, so that encouraged me. I put it on the summer before my first year in middle school. I remember being very nervous on the first day of school. The kids had a lot of stupid questions like 'When you take a shower do you take it off? 'Were you born with it on?' Just funny things. I didn't know how much I could tell them about my religion when I responded."

When I commented on how difficult that must have been, Noor shook her head. "No, there were advantages. I was the only one in the school who wore hijab, so everybody knew who I was. They all said 'Hi' to me. When I was a member of Diversity Council at school, I had the opportunity to tell them why I was wearing hijab. I told them that it doesn't have anything to do with oppressing women. In fact, it's empowering. It's a form of not letting men objectify women for their hair, their outside beauty. I wanted people to know what I was like inside, not just the outside. The students responded and understood. I think I did a good job. It was a journey, and I had a choice. My parents didn't tell me to wear hijab, and that makes me even more attached to it."

I was speechless. Noor's maturity was amazing. In my wide acquaintance with Muslim women, I had never heard anyone express their reasons for wearing the head scarf as well as this fifteen-year-old girl.

Her strength of belief in the importance of donning the head scarf was evident when Nisren told me about asking Noor to go outside one night to get something from their backyard. Neither Noor nor Nisren wore the head scarf in the house when only the family was present. Noor's response wasn't the typical teen-age refusal to take out the trash. She said, "No, I can't do that because someone will see me."

"It's dark. No one will see you," her mother replied.

"That doesn't matter. Allah will see me."

Observing her daughter's confidence had informed her mother's ability to answer questions from people who were curious about her long dress and the hijab that covered her hair. She told me about one day when she was volunteering at the used book sale at Bemis Library. A boy asked a question about the way she dressed. "It's part of my religion," Nisren told him. "It protects a woman and saves her appearance for her special person, her husband."

Unfortunately, Mohammed wasn't able to be in on our discussion of first days because there were classes at his middle school, but according to his mom, he was a laid-back second grader when they first enrolled him in school. He learned spoken English quickly and enjoyed tasting both the new food and practicing the idioms of the culture. Both Noor and Nisren started giggling. They recalled his enthusiasm about a wonderful new food he had tried in the school cafeteria one day.

"I had a stick with some food, not meat, on the end. It was delicious, so I ate two of them," he told his mom.

"Oh, Mohammed, that was a hot dog. It was *haram*," Nisren responded. Haram, forbidden, applies to pork and all meat products that have not been slaughtered or prepared in a manner proscribed by Islamic law. The term *halal* means the opposite: food is permissible or approved. The solution for Mohammed's culinary adventure was to ask the school for vegetarian meals or to make lunch for him to take to school. Mohammed also discovered Chipotle restaurant food, which he brought home to Nisren, so now she fixes Mexican food that is halal.

Noor wanted to hear more of what her mother had to say about adjusting to American culture. After getting a glass of juice from the kitchen, she returned to a chair in the living room. Nisren described the first year as filled with challenges: the children's adjustment to school, English classes, cooking with ingredients that were sometimes hard to find, Raad's work at the auto dealership, and just absorbing the newness of the surroundings and the culture. In spite of the busyness of daily life, there was always a pall of loneliness that hung over her while they were living in the small two-bedroom apartment. After getting a cell phone, Nisren would call her family in Baghdad every morning and she would cry, not just a few tears but audible sobs.

"I always had the windows open when I was on the telephone, and I know I talked loudly." She explained that the man next door drank all night and slept during the day. When he heard her crying, he knocked on the door and shouted for her to be quiet. Another neighbor, a woman who had become Nisren's friend, came out of her apartment to defend her. "My neighbor told him I was far away from my family and was homesick. I apologized to the man, and he was nice to me. After that, I still cried, but I kept the windows closed when I called home."

Her loneliness and homesickness didn't lessen as the months passed; they deepened into depression. The children were in school, Raad was at work, and she was alone in the apartment all day except for the few hours when she would go to the library for an ESL class. Littleton had no Iraqi community, so she was isolated from other immigrants and refugees who were experiencing similar feelings.

Noor looked surprised when she heard her mother talk about the loneliness she had experienced. Although they were very close, she hadn't realized how serious her mother's situation was. She reached over to put her hand on Nisren's knee. Her mom turned and directed her explanation directly to Noor. "Sometimes when I was alone at home, I just couldn't forget what happened in Baghdad. The memories came back and most of the time I cried. Until now I'm scared to leave the door unlocked. Many times when I'm upstairs in bed and I can't sleep, I imagine someone coming in. I didn't feel that way at first. I felt safe and one hundred percent without worry. After a while, when I watched violence on Egyptian daytime serials or the TV news, I remembered everything, and I was afraid again."

As she shared how she felt in those early years, I heard all the symptoms of post-traumatic stress disorder (PTSD), the mental health condition experienced by multitudes of military veterans. PTSD is triggered by experiencing or witnessing terrifying events accompanied by symptoms of flashbacks, nightmares, and severe anxiety, as well as uncontrollable thoughts about those events. This definition fit Nisren's experience in the early stages of her adjustment. I wished Mika, Susan, and I had sensed what she was going through. She appeared to us to be happy and adapting well to the new culture. Those of us who were interacting with her then should have recognized the warning signs, so we could have made more of an effort to connect her with the Iraqi community and to offer professional help. It is a lesson for anyone working with refugees and immigrants from war-torn countries. Her support system in Iraq was her family. She shared every joy and difficulty with them. There was no one in the isolation of this Denver suburb to replace the extended family at home in Baghdad. The members of the community at the mosque they helped to start should have served that purpose, but their involvement ended several years after they came because, as Nisren explained, "There was too much drama with other Iraqis, and sometimes they didn't show enough respect for their new country and its laws. I miss some of the families, but it's better this way." Cutting off their contacts with other Iraqis at the mosque was a serious, principled decision, especially since maintaining that connection was a way for the children to keep in touch with their culture and religion. Mohammed, in particular, still missed the Muslim friends he had made, who no longer spoke to him or contacted him.

Added to the family's worries was a workplace accident that injured Raad's hand, so he could no longer do car repair. The auto company offered him only $15,000 in workmen's compensation, but he was no longer able to receive the more lucrative mechanic's salary. Mika talked to a workmen's compensation attorney but was told that it might take years to fight the claim. Raad decided to take the money offered. The auto company also paid him a mechanic's salary for a year.

His job gave them just enough to survive on. These problems could not be ignored, but they were balanced by positive accomplishments. They were achieving their main purpose in immigrating to the United States: a safe, secure environment for their family and the opportunity for their children to thrive and receive a good education. The children were on the plus side of the adjustment equation. Mohammed was a friendly, popular student in an elementary school that had children from many countries. Noor was stimulated by her ability to learn and achieve good grades, and she was making friends. Raad had employment related to his automotive job in Iraq, opposed to other refugees who found it difficult to find any job with relevance to the past.

A computer and a television set, important for any new immigrant, eased their homesickness. The computer allowed them to share face-time with their families at home in Iraq, and an online software package allowed them to watch Iraqi programming on their TV. This kept them in touch with Iraqi news, music, and even cartoons in Arabic. It also kept the children's cultural roots alive.

When Nisren mentioned the importance of seeing Iraqi programs, Noor rolled her eyes accompanied by a one-word comment: "Really?" Nisren countered by reminding her of when they watched a recent TV special about Saddam Hussein.

"You were horrified when you saw children reading admiring poems to Saddam," Nisren said. "I told you that you were like this as a toddler. You kissed and hugged the TV saying, 'I love Saddam.' We taught you to say this to protect you and our family."

This reminder of the past didn't change Noor's expression of disdain. She viewed her response to Saddam's face on TV as childish without realizing the dire implications of not praising the dictator. At the time, this innocence protected her from the trauma adult family members were experiencing.

The solution to Nisren's loneliness came in their third year in the US. She was pregnant and happily so. Raad was excited, too. However, paying for prenatal care was problematic. Raad's work provided health insurancefor him, but it was too expensive to include Nisren. Luckily, the children had health care through the Children's Health Insurance Program (CHIP). Prior to becoming pregnant, Nisren had used Doctors Care, a private nonprofit clinic that offered health access for low-income individuals in the south metro Denver area. Payment at this clinic was made on a sliding scale of income. But when she became pregnant, more specialized pre-natal care was needed for Nisren because she would require a Caesarean section and treatment for possible gestational diabetes. Again, Mika stepped in to help. She researched the local services and found that financial assistance would be provided for Nisren if she visited the Women's Care Clinic at Denver Health Medical Center.

Nisren and Mika had already faced cultural quirks the first time they visited Doctors Care. Nisren had been ushered into an exam room where a male nurse asked her to disrobe while he stepped out. In Iraq, only female nurses see women patients. This was one cultural adjustment she wasn't ready for. She rushed out to the waiting room for help. Mika interceded, and a female nurse stepped in. When it came time to visit the Women's Care Clinic, Mika asked in advance for a female nurse and doctor. The clinic was able to oblige, and Nisren was pleased with the professional attention she received. However, at the conclusion of the appointment, she was informed that she had gestational diabetes requiring special precautions during the pregnancy. Then she and Mika were asked to see a genetic counselor, who shocked both of them by saying, "Because of your age and diabetes, you have a 30-40 percent chance of having a baby with a disability." Down syndrome was mentioned as an example. Nisren, who was only 32 at the time, was stunned. "I told her there had never been anything like this in my family." The counselor suggested she have another test to decide whether or not to terminate the pregnancy. On the return trip home, Mika and Nisren discussed the frightening news. Mika told her she needed to talk to Raad and decide together whether or not to proceed with the pregnancy. "It doesn't matter what you decide, but it does matter that you both agree," she counseled.

When Nisren came home, she was crying, "not for me, but for the baby." She managed to have the report translated, so she could understand the recommendations. She also researched Down syndrome and was encouraged by what she found. "These babies are like angels on earth when I see how they act," she concluded. When Raad returned from work, she shared the news and her research with him.

Raad's reply was, "A baby is a gift from God. You don't say, 'Allah, I don't want a baby.' You want to keep it, no matter what."

Their decision was confirmed several weeks later when a doctor performed an amniocentesis procedure, extracting amniotic fluid to determine any genetic abnormalities such as Down syndrome. The test showed no abnormalities. The journey to the birth of a third child had begun. Even a diagnosis of gestational diabetes did not dampen Nisren's enthusiasm about her pregnancy, although extra doctor visits and close monitoring of her blood sugar were required. Mika accompanied the mother-to-be to almost all of her appointments because Nisren did not drive, and Raad was often unable to take time off from work at the auto dealership. Other than the initial shock of a possible abortion and the diabetes diagnosis, both the pre-natal care and birth were delightful to Nisren. There was no comparing her difficult pregnancies and frightening deliveries in Baghdad to the personal attention and encouragement she received in the United States. Another huge difference was that Raad got to be part of the delivery.

"The birth of the baby was wonderful," she said. "I was awake every second during the birth. I didn't feel any pain. I loved the whole process. I felt so close to Raad, who held my hand through the whole delivery. Raad even asked me if he could record the birth on his phone, but I said 'no.'"

Mika visited Nisren and the baby in the hospital and immediately commented, "I have never seen a more beautiful baby!" Nisren agreed: "Imagine! We had a picture of the baby after he was cleaned up. He was our love child,"

They named their son Hussein, meaning "beautiful or handsome," after the grandson of the Prophet Muhammad.

CHAPTER 6

Citizenship

Nisren was radiant as the mother of a newborn. From the time she cared for her baby sister Venos in Iraq to the births of Noor and Mohammed, she had loved nurturing babies. Now her loneliness slipped into the background as the immediate needs of a new baby happily filled her time. Her relationship with Raad also had developed into a new closeness.

"We talked more, and he shared his feelings more often. I think seeing close relationships among American couples changed him. Also, in America, he had no one but me and the kids to pay attention to. In Iraq, he was busy with all his siblings, cousins, and friends."

Their fifth year in the US was a banner year for the family: They were granted American citizenship, which provided new opportunities, and the family was growing and thriving. In 2014, Noor graduated from middle school and Mohammed completed elementary school. These are important accomplishments for all children but even more so for immigrants who have had to learn English and adapt to a new culture.

My husband and I attended Noor's graduation from Goddard Middle School, an attractive one story building close to Littleton's historic Main Street. Goddard serves about 750 students in grades six through eight. It was a cloudy day in May when we searched for a parking space in the packed school parking lot. Although we were twenty minutes early, the gymnasium was overflowing with families of many ethnicities. I learned later that fifty-seven percent of Goddard's kids were white, thirty-five percent Hispanic, and the remainder other nationalities. Luckily, a couple with two small children scooped them up on their laps and offered us a seat. We heard someone in the stands yelling "Connie! Connie!" and looked up to the top of the risers to see Mohammed shouting at us and Raad and Nisren, holding Hussein, proudly waving their hands. When Noor received her certificate, loud applause and a few shouts came from her family. When the ceremony was finished, we congratulated her and met her best friend, an Ethiopian girl who had studied with her since elementary school.

Soon after Noor's completion of middle school, Raad and Nisren celebrated their US citizenship. They had met the requirements of five years continuous residency in the United States and had "good moral character," meaning they had not committed any offenses and had no criminal records. Before the official fifth anniversary of their admission to the US, they had been studying hard for the naturalization test, which covers 100 questions about important US history and government topics. During the interview process, applicants are asked up to 10 questions and must be able to answer at least 6 of them correctly. They had memorized answers to questions like these: Who is in charge of the executive branch? What is the Bill of Rights? How many voting members are in the House of Representatives? How many changes or amendments to the Constitution are there? Who becomes President if both the President and Vice-President die? They breezed through a test that, I believe, many native-born Americans might fail.

Amid the waving of small US flags and speeches from local officials in the Littleton Municipal Building, they took the oath of allegiance to the United States and stood to listen to the singing of the national anthem and "America the Beautiful." Becoming a citizen offered several benefits: the right to vote and be elected to office, priority in petitioning for relatives to join them in the United States, the ability to travel freely with a US passport, eligibility for Federal jobs, the opportunity to become an elected official, and the right to collect benefits, such as Social Security and Medicare. Hussein, who was born in the United States, was automatically a US citizen. Mohammed and Noor, who were both under 18, gained citizenship when their parents were naturalized.

"Citizenship was a dream for us. As soon as I got here, I felt I was from here, but sometimes people outside see you as different. But now I know that as a citizen, I'm really an American," Nisren said. The knowledge that she legally was a citizen gave her strength and courage. She recalled an incident from the past when she was judged, she believes, because she was wearing a long dress and a hijab.

"When we were shopping for groceries in King Soopers, I noticed an employee following us through the store," Nisren related. When Raad turned and asked him what was wrong, he explained that it was his job to prevent shoplifting. "After Raad explained who we were, he apologized for being suspicious of our actions. I remember thinking if I had my citizenship, I would have complained and stood up for myself. Citizenship gave me that power."

It also gave the family permission to travel freely outside the US, an important privilege for Raad and Nisren. They were desperate to see their families again, so they immediately applied for passports to travel as soon as possible to visit Baghdad. In the middle of their preparations, Nisren received the bad news that her father, who was 65, had died suddenly from illness related to kidney disease. She had been so close to seeing him again before he died.

"It was a hard time," she said. "When I think of him, I remember those times as a little kid when we went every day to the park and the whole family lived together in the big apartment house."

Realizing the fragility of their parents' lives made Raad and Nisren even more eager to visit them as soon as possible. They would switch off on their trips. While Nisren took care of the family, Raad would spend six weeks in Iraq. Nisren would have the opportunity to travel as soon as he returned.

Unfortunately, this wasn't the longed-for return Raad had hoped for after five years. "I couldn't show my face in my neighborhood," he said. "I had to go in the night time to see my mom because people would still be able to identify me. If someone had been hurt by Americans, they would never forget that I was an interpreter there."

It was difficult for him to understand why Iraqis hated the interpreters. "People thought I was doing this just because I knew English. They're wrong. All of us, doctors, professors, and pilots were interpreting because we loved our country and wanted to help change it." His biggest disappointment was in the Iraq he saw on his visit. "I wanted to see changes for the better," he said. "If I could tell the people, the police, the councils, I would say 'You're liars. You're destroying Iraq. Don't cheat. Don't steal weapons and give them to the militia.'"

UN statistics give frightening reality to the conditions Raad observed. Since the family immigrated in 2009, executions, car bombs, assassinations, artillery shelling, and aerial bombardment had killed and injured more than 20,000 civilians. Pro-government militias had carried out assassinations, property destruction, and kidnappings. Since the time of their immigration, the conflict had displaced nearly 3.2 million Iraqis and interrupted school for more than three million children as well as access to medical care, food, and clean water.

Along with Raad's secretive visits to his family members came their demands to bring them to the United States to live. Under US law citizens could sponsor their spouses, children, parents, and siblings for family visas, also known as "green cards," depending on their age and marital status. When Raad returned from his visit in 2015, it was still possible for Iraqis to obtain visas. However, his family did not understand that application for a green card was a lengthy, complicated process with improbable results. In spite of these restrictions, Raad began the detailed process of sponsoring them for family visas. As a sponsor, he had to file a petition proving his relationship and submit a signed affidavit of support showing financial responsibility for each applicant. On the slim chance that the application for Iraqi family members would be accepted, they would have to submit lengthy applications, go through extensive background and security checks, including criminal, national security, health-related and other screenings. If US Citizenship and Immigration Services (USCIS) approved the petition, it would be forwarded to the National Visa Center, which directs the applicant to complete certain forms, submit documents, and pay the fees. Once this is received, a US embassy or consulate officer conducts an interview to determine his or her eligibility. Then the applicant has to undergo a medical examination and obtain necessary vaccinations before the government will issue a visa. And how long does this process take? Years or even decades, based on an applicant's relationship with his or her sponsor.

In researching the multitude of steps involved in obtaining a family visa, I realized the relatively simple process immigration must have been for my own ancestors. My maternal grandfather emigrated from Denmark sponsored only by a close friend who would help him to settle and work in Minnesota. He later married my grandmother, the child of Norwegian immigrants. My paternal grandfather arrived from Sweden by himself but brought his wife and child a year later, an example of the "chain migration" that has been the primary basis for immigration to the United States since colonial times. It was formally approved in 1965 by The Immigration and Nationality Act. Family visas have accounted for about 65 percent of legal immigration each year, but this may change if immigration reform takes place in the future. Hopefully, reform will recognize the economic benefits among the many gifts these new Americans and their communities bring with them.

Raad understood the difficulties of obtaining visas for his close family members, but he felt the commitment to giving them some sliver of hope to escape the dangers and stagnation of life in Iraq. He also discovered that his immigration to America meant losing the power to control what happens in his family back home. He had sent money to assist his aging mother but discovered this same money had been used for birthday parties for the children of his siblings. In addition, his investment in the family auto repair business was being used by his brothers instead of being returned to him. "I didn't feel like I belonged. Instead of being part of the family, I was a guest, someone who would come and go away again."

Nisren's turn came next. She was not under suspicion as Raad had been. She would be able to see her parents and extended family and to bring Hussein with her, so they could meet her newest addition to the family. It was the custom to bring gifts from the US for each family member or at least for the children, but Nisren did not know the sizes for clothes and actually did not have money for gifts, so she didn't take anything with her. This caused some problems because "everyone thinks if you come from America, you're rich." Nisren didn't realize how difficult it would be for a three-year-old to travel to strange surroundings and be engulfed in cultural customs he didn't understand. "Hussein didn't like Iraq. His relatives wanted to touch his long hair. He didn't want to play with his cousins, and he didn't speak Arabic or Kurdish. Every day we had to visit a different house. He cried and hid behind me, and he also missed his dad so much."

Her family immediately took stock of her appearance and her attitudes to determine how she might have changed. In a sense, she was on trial, and the answers to their many questions produced judgments. "How come you've gotten religious? You're wearing hijab and going to the mosque. You should go to night clubs and have fun. What's happened to you? You're crazy not to do these things" were comments made by relatives. They thought it would be easier for her to dress American style, but she told them, "I wouldn't feel like *me* if I didn't wear my hijab. It's just part of me."

Nisren had expected her family to be interested in her new life in the US and tell her how much they missed her, just as she had missed them. But instead of a warm welcome, she discovered through her visits to various family members that some relatives had talked about her behind her back, criticizing the short time she stayed at each of their houses. She just couldn't please all of them. Within a few days, she was struck by all the changes in Iraqi life since she had left. She didn't see the diversity of Christians, Jews, and Muslims she had enjoyed as a child. Everyone seemed divided into different ethnic camps: Shia and Sunni and Kurdish. People were more afraid and tense. "When I was a little girl, we didn't even lock our doors. Now it's more dangerous than when we left. You do what you have to do outside and then come back home fast because you may not come back at all," she commented. One of the most shocking differences between her American life and the lives of family members was how children were being educated. She described to her relatives Noor and Mohammed's first year in an American school with two teachers who "welcomed them, cared about them, and individually helped them learn English." She observed her Iraqi nieces and nephews doing page after page of useless homework that their teachers never reviewed or even looked at. It was common to hire a teacher as an after-school tutor because children didn't learn enough at school to be able to pass their exams. This practice also benefited teachers' incomes. "A lot of kids had lost their fathers during the wars, so families didn't often have enough money to give children simple things that teachers require, like crayons, paper, and scissors," she told me. In fact, a simple pair of scissors became an issue with her sister's daughter. "Because she didn't bring a pair of scissors to class, the teacher gave her a bad grade and hit her on both sides of her head," Nisren said. When the little girl came home crying and didn't want to return to school, her mother complained to the teacher, who confronted her: "Maybe I'll have to hit *you*, not the girl."

Unlike Raad's family, Nisren's had no desire to come to America. Instead they asked her why she didn't come back to Iraq to live. She answered, "The US is my home. I'm 100 percent sure the future of my kids and my future is there."

Her trip also clarified the dangers her family faced in Iraq. "Before it was just one Saddam to be afraid of, but now there are many Saddams, stealing money and bombing. Last week I heard there was a bombing in our old neighborhood at 7 a.m. The people who were killed were the poor who have to go to work every day early in the morning. I'm more scared for my family than they are. They tell me their problems are nothing when they try to convince me to come home." Just a year after her travel, Nisren's mother died from a heart attack and complications of diabetes. She had been blessed with the opportunity to see her mother before her death, but it was a shock to lose both parents. She expressed her grief by donning a black hijab and abaya, not just for the required three days of mourning after the death of a parent but for an entire year. "I don't like to wear black, but I wanted to show respect for my father and mother."

Some comfort for her grief came from her firm belief in life after death, which is a foundational truth in Islam. Grief should be processed with the understanding that death is not the end of life but a transition to an eternal one. Nisren also found solace in old friends from the mosque who contacted her even though her family had stopped participating in religious gatherings. When I asked her how her beliefs had helped her throughout all the trials in her life, she responded with a newly-acquired American idiom: "I always feel that Allah has my back. He is always with me. When I have to make decisions or need help, I say a special prayer, the *Salat-L-Istikhara*. God knows what is best for me," she said.

CHAPTER 7

What Do You Do When They Call You a Terrorist?

A YEAR LATER, IN THE MIDDLE OF THE 2016 PRESIDENTIAL CAMPAIGNS, I WAS SITTING ACROSS FROM NISREN AND NOOR AT A PICNIC TABLE IN A LITTLETON PARK. We had invited all the immigrants who had been given grants from our Immigrant Pathways Colorado group to enjoy a picnic lunch together. Raad and Mohammed were playing volleyball, and Hussein was running back and forth between the game and blowing bubbles at our table. It had been several months since I had visited with the family, so I was eager for an update after their citizenship and travel to Iraq.

Nisren and Noor were enjoying the sunshine and watching the kids on the playground nearby. They had contributed two special Iraqi dishes to the buffet table in the picnic shelter. They had lemonade glasses in front of them but no food in spite of the abundance of kosher hot dogs cooked on the grill.

I asked them if they felt any different now that they were US citizens.

"We're happy that we can vote now—and not for Donald Trump," Nisren said. "In the seven years we've been here, I've never had any bad things happen to me. Of course, when you look or dress different, people sometimes judge you before knowing you." Evidently the scarf and long dress that protected her from scrutiny and was a sign of respect had become an object of derision. She nervously laughed when she described what to me was a very hurtful incident but one that proved she was culturally aware.

"One day when I came out of the supermarket to get in the car with Raad, someone shouted 'Go back to your country' and a couple of guys 'gave me the finger,'" she said with a defiant shrug of her shoulders. "I was both mad and scared at the same time."

Noor, a junior in high school with a 4.5 grade average, had been very quiet until this moment. The transition from girl- to woman-hood was evident in her expressive long-lashed eyes and her slim, oval face. She nudged her mom with her elbow.

"Tell Connie about what happened to Mohammed."

Nisren described an incident he experienced in the last few months of middle school. Mohammed came home crying and wanted to quit school. Although he didn't want to give his mother any details, he finally opened up and told her about a fight with a boy in his seventh grade class.

"Mohammed's a terrorist name, and you look like one! Fatty! Black eyebrows! Terrorist!" the bully had shouted at him. This wasn't a one-time incident. Some girls had started calling Mohammed names and showing their friends a video of ISIS men with black flags. Then they engaged the boys in the same actions. Mohammed had suffered some shoves and punches in the hallways and tried to ignore them, but the bully's name-calling was the final insult. He punched the boy and in the ensuing fight, gave him a black eye. When teachers intervened, the bully said Mohammed had started the fight. When Nisren heard the story, her anger pushed her into calling the principal who reassured her that the school counselor would talk to the boy and to Mohammed. If the problem wasn't solved, he promised he would involve the parents. Although the principal never called Nisren with a report, the bullying stopped, but within the next week, another incident happened.

"I knew something was wrong because after school Mohammed would just go upstairs to his bedroom and was mad all the time. This scared me because he used to love school. Again, I talked with the principal and his teachers and found out that a teacher had accused him of stealing." The story unfolded when a girl had asked Mohammed to help open her locker because the door was stuck. His math teacher saw him pulling on the locker door and assumed he was trying to get into the locker to take something. After meeting with Mohammed, the teacher, and the girl, the real story came out. Notes of apology were sent to Nisren and Raad. The teacher told Nisren that he "loved Mohammed in class" but had seen him in the fight and had mistaken his intent with the locker. Later the teacher apologized directly to Mohammed, but this didn't ease the pain he felt, especially because the teacher was his favorite. Now when Mohammed sees the bullies on the school grounds, he goes out of his way to avoid them. Luckily, most of them are not continuing to the same high school.

Mohammed's experience wasn't an isolated incident. According to a 2017 Pew Research Center survey, Muslims in the United States perceived a pattern of discrimination against their religious group. They were distrustful of the current administration and thought their fellow Americans did not see Islam as part of mainstream American society. The same survey showed that those with distinctively Muslim appearance, such as women wearing hijab, were more likely to experience name-calling, being singled out by law enforcement, or being physically attacked or threatened.

As I pursued our topic of the country's growing resentment toward immigrants created by the Presidential campaign, Nisren told me that her family in Baghdad had been following the news and discussed the debate about immigration with them in their weekly

Skype conversations. Always ready to see the humor in difficult times, she commented, "My sisters were happy because they thought we would be sent back to Iraq if Trump became president, but my brother told me not to make any mistakes because Trump might tell us to go home where we belong."

Our picnic table conversation was followed a few months later by another conversation after the inauguration of President Trump. His executive order banning immigrants from mostly Muslim countries, including Iraq, produced fear in immigrants from those countries. It also stimulated negative responses from Americans who saw these people as a threat. Nasty words and gestures by passersby plagued Nisren and the children, but they continued to use their new citizenship as a shield that gave them strength in their right to be in the United States. It also was comforting to Raad and Nisren to hear support from Colorado's lieutenant governor Donna Lynne, who called on President Trump to rescind his executive order, and Governor John Hickenlooper, who said refugees have "navigated through the world's most stringent and toughest vetting system" and that the nation does not need "religious tests and blanket bans that contradict the basic values this country was built on."

Although I continued to visit the family regularly as a friend, it was time for some wrap-up questions as a journalist. It was a few weeks after Christmas, but the previous day's 35 degree temperature had climbed to a pleasant 70 degrees, typical Colorado swings in the weather. The small concrete porch in front of the duplex had been swept clean and the broken bench taken away. When Nisren and Hussein opened the door to me, I was greeted by a new Persian-style carpet, a 48-inch TV on a stand that featured an electric fireplace, and two parakeets in a cage. The light from the fireplace illuminated a spread of goodies on the coffee table, waiting for me: tangerines, nuts, and a tall glass of juice. I was reminded that Christmas for this

Muslim family was observed as a secular holiday in Iraq. "We used to decorate a tree and give small gifts," Nisren told me. That holiday atmosphere was apparent in their home in Colorado today.

Five-year-old Hussein, who just missed the cut-off date for kindergarten, had made a somewhat difficult transition from being home with Nisren to being surrounded by a noisy bunch of kids at a nearby public preschool. "He's growing up too fast," Nisren confided. "Sometimes when I hug him if he's sleeping next to me, I wish he were still my baby." Hussein interrupted to pull me into the kitchen to look at the two colorful little birds. Nisren scolded him, as he poked at them through the bars of the cage and tried to imitate their cooing. "He's not the quiet baby anymore," she said. "Now he's noisy and full of energy no matter how long he sleeps."

Before we settled down to talk about the changes in their lives, Hussein asked for a piece of paper from my notebook and showed me how he could print his name. He pressed hard on his pencil to print an orderly group of letters that spelled out "Hussein." He accepted my praise with pride and told me that his best friend in school was a girl named Giarda. "Tell Connie what your favorite things are in school," his mom said. "Hmm," he said thoughtfully. "I like playing and, oh yeah, story time."

"Hussein is such an American kid," Nisren said. "He's 100 percent different from Noor and Mohammed. He stands up to his dad when Raad corrects his behavior and says, 'You are the mean boy. Not me.' It's different from how I showed respect for my dad. When he was angry, I hid and asked my mom to talk to him. After he had cooled down, I would go and talk to him, eyes down, but not Hussein."

Mohammed was now 16 and Noor 17. Being teenagers creates significant changes in all children, but I wondered if these two adolescents had been affected even more by the immigrant experience. When I posed this question, Nisren told me she was surprised at how much more open and stronger both kids were after going through adjustments here. "Noor used to be shy," she said, "but now she is confident, talks openly, and shares everything with me." Their close relationship was admirable. Not many moms of teenage girls could attest to this candor.

I worried that Mohammed had not recovered from the middle school bullying, but Nisren told me he was showing signs of the happy-go-lucky kid he used to be, who liked school and would even do his homework as long as he could listen to music and watch videos at the same time. She told me that Raad calls him a genius because he can do three things at once. Mohammed's cultural adjustment had its positives and its negatives. He was intrigued the first time some years ago when he saw a couple kissing on TV. "Look what they're doing, Mom," he shouted. He was curious about what was going on between the man and woman because he had never even seen his parents kiss which, in their culture, would be done in private only. Nisren saw the humor in this. "He's used to it now, but that makes me worry more about him than I do about Noor."

In spite of, or maybe because of, the American freedom of choice, she was raising her children very much as she was raised. "My parents were close to us, and they didn't shout or lecture. They gave us choices. Even though our grandmothers on both sides of the family were sisters, my dad wanted me to make my own decision about marriage. I could have said "No" to Raad if I didn't think he was the best choice. If Noor makes a choice to marry someone who's not Kurdish, that's OK with us. Her cousins at home think she must marry Kurdish. But my hopes for the kids are that they get a good education, be what they want to be, and have a better life than we did. I want them to live in peace and never go to sleep hungry. I hope they can own a house. In Iraq, we all dreamed of owning a house but couldn't."

"And what about you, Nisren?" I asked. "What changes have you been through?" As she considered the question, she paused, looked across the room at Hussein who was playing with his brother's old smart phone, and turned back to me.

"I saw a lot of American movies at home, so I thought I knew a lot about American people, but I didn't have any idea about women's rights," she said. "I hadn't imagined how much respect there was for women here. Women are number one in America." She explained how seeing this regard for women had changed Raad's attitude. "He has become more understanding of my feelings and tells me how much he appreciates me. I knew he loved me before, but now he can talk about love. He listened to me before but didn't take my opinions and ideas as seriously. He listens to Noor, too, and treats her as a special person."

I took a sip of juice as she considered other changes in herself. Then I recalled the confidence and strength I had seen her gain over the years. When I saw her struggling with adjustment and loneliness, I never would have believed she could stand in front of an audience of more than 50 people, holding a microphone, and speaking about her immigrant experience. And yet, she did exactly that as one of three panelists at a luncheon for donors to Immigrant Pathways Colorado. At the luncheon before the panel discussion, Nisren and Hussein were seated at a table with Mika, who was prepared with toys to take Hussein outside during the program if he got restless. Also at the table were several donors and another woman wearing hijab. It was Eman, the other subject of interviews for this book. This was the first time for the two women to meet. They enjoyed talking about their families and their new lives in the US. Nisren joined two other immigrants on the panel, a Venezuelan and a Peruvian. As the moderator, I encouraged each woman to tell her story. As Nisren talked about her life in Iraq and the journey of being an immigrant in the US, I saw tears in the eyes of audience members. She described her family's hardships and the hope they found in America. When I asked the three panelists "Why did you want to become citizens?" Nisren quickly replied, "I wanted to vote for president and have the power to stand up for myself in all situations." After the discussion, Nisren was blushing with pride when people from the audience praised her performance, but most importantly, she stopped to show me a text message Raad had sent to her smart phone when he left for work in the morning. "It was the first time for me to see these words in writing," she whispered. The message said, "Good luck. I love you."

There were many blessings in this family's lives. But of course, some things did not change. The experience of living more than half her life in fear didn't vanish when Nisren came to the United States. Sometimes during my visits, I felt that she was trying too hard to please me by being positive about everything, but during out final interview, she seemed ready to tell me about the other side of the coin: the emotional and psychological bruises from years spent under the cloud of a war-mongering, evil dictator. These fears may have lessened, but they did not disappear with time.

"How do the difficulties of your life in Baghdad affect you now?" I asked.

She looked at me directly and didn't hesitate. "Almost never have I lived in peace and security. Instead, I've always lived with fear. Saddam was president when I was born. But even now, I'm scared to leave the door unlocked. Sometimes when I'm upstairs and can't sleep, I think I see someone coming into the room. I didn't feel that way in our first days here because everything was new, wonderful, and safe. I didn't have to worry at all. Then we got the connection to television channels in Iraq and others in the Middle East. At times, I would remember everything, and I was afraid again."

I remembered a recent experience that triggered her fear. Nisren was taking Hussein on a short walk to the park near the duplex soon after President Trump had issued an executive order banning entry of foreign nationals from Iraq and six other Muslim countries for 90 days, She hadn't ventured out of the house without Raad for more than a month because of the fear of Muslims that pervaded the news. Two cars slowly drove by them with the men inside honking and shouting, "Go back where you belong! Terrorist!" Nisren tried to ignore them but was afraid that they might harm her and Hussein, so she turned and walked quickly down a path into the park. A woman jogging in the park saw what was happening and yelled back at the men to stop the harassment and go away. Then she came up to Nisren and Hussein and apologized: "I'm sorry there are people like that."

When I mentioned this incident, she replied with typical compassion and fairness. "When that happened to me, I thought maybe those guys had been hurt by a Muslim or were soldiers in the war. They must have had a reason for what they did."

Before interviewing Nisren, I did not realize the power fear can have over a person. Her story was a testimony to that power, a force that can fence in a life, restrict one's daily activities, and limit a person's dreams. Her story also attests to the strength that can arise in the face of adversity and the hope that can come with life in a free country.

"Connie, Connie, come see me feed the birds," Hussein shouted. I turned off the recorder and walked into the immaculate kitchen. The sun was shining directly on the birdcage through the big kitchen window. The yellow and blue parakeets cocked their heads at the overly enthusiastic five-year-old. I noticed that one of the birds had lost a few feathers due to Hussein's curiosity. His mother helped him put a tiny bit of bird seed in the feeder attached to the cage.

Nisren gave him a hug and turned to me. "You know, Connie, what helps me the most to not be afraid?"

I shook my head.

"Every night before I go to sleep, I think about everything and thank God I got here and that my family is safe. I see my kids and my husband next to me, and I don't want anything else from this life."

CHAPTER 8

Postscript

I WASN'T FINISHED YET. NISREN'S STORY HAD BEEN TOLD FROM HER VIEWPOINT AS A WIFE AND MOTHER, BUT I NEEDED TO BALANCE THIS WITH RAAD'S PERSPECTIVE AS A FORMER INTERPRETER WHO MADE THE DECISION TO TAKE HIS FAMILY TO THE UNITED STATES. It was a Sunday afternoon in June in the middle of Ramadan when I went to their home to visit with Raad, the first time I had formally interviewed him. Nisren and Hussein met me at the door. The minute I stepped inside, I heard Raad angrily shouting from the kitchen in Kurdish. This was not his inside voice. It must have been the volume and tone he used to control the crowd during the first day of the American invasion. But what was happening now? When Nisren greeted me, she explained that her husband was on the phone with his brother in Baghdad unsuccessfully trying to convince him to take the family out of the country as soon as possible.

I tried to ignore Raad's impassioned voice and focus on Nisren and Hussein. It was the first time I had seen Nisren without a hijab and wearing a long, short-sleeved American-style dress. Her long black hair, streaked with a bit of gray, was clasped behind her neck. In spite of Raad's shouting, she was relaxed and filled with good news. Noor, who had graduated from Littleton high school that week, had received a full scholarship to the University of Colorado at Denver with the goal of becoming a dentist. Graduation photos on Nisren's smart phone showed a smiling young woman wearing a red jumpsuit peeking out from her purple gown, her hijab topped by a mortarboard. On this day, she was out of the house at a graduation party with her Ethiopian girlfriend. Hussein, who was his usual impish self, interrupted to tell me about his achievements. With a dramatic sweep of his arm, he said, "I'm going to kindergarten, but it's going to be hard. I'm really, really scared." Mohammed, whom I hadn't seen in person for several years, came thumping down the stairs. I had to reach up a foot to give him a hug. He was just an inch or so taller than his dad and eager to talk about anything but his up-and-coming third year in high school. When we had difficulty hearing each other over Raad's demanding conversation, Mohammed laughed. He tromped into the kitchen to tell his dad to go outside to finish his call. When he returned, he updated me about school. "I'm a junior now. It's supposed to be the hardest year yet." He hadn't decided what he wanted to study in college but was thinking about being a diplomat because a teacher told him he could use his abilities in three languages if he made this choice. Mohammed was also proud to report that he had his first job as a lifeguard at Pirate's Cove, a water park near the house. He had learned to swim in a high school class.

Raad finished his conversation and covered the space from the backdoor into the living room in several long strides. The small room now sported three short sofas arranged in a conversation group. Nisren had inched forward on the one opposite me. Raad stood by where I was seated for a few seconds, trying to calm down with several deep breaths. He leaned down and gave me a quick embrace. Then he nervously sat down the edge of the empty sofa. This was not the best time to interview him, I worried. For one thing, he didn't quite understand what the interviews and the book were about, and for another, he was focused on events in Iraq, not here in Colorado.

"I've been trying to tell my brother he has to leave Iraq with the family now," he emphasized with a thump of his fist on the sofa arm.

"Iraq is zero. No more. Now the big lie has become the truth."

"Iraq is done," Nisren echoed from across the room.

"The militia who destroyed the country and started the war now leads the government."

Raad was referring to Muqhtada al-Sadr, the influential Shiite cleric whose political coalition won a plurality in Iraq's national elections May 18, 2018. Al-Sadr had become the de facto leader of the Iraqi nation. He wouldn't become prime minister, but he would control the formation of the next Iraqi government. It was al-Sadr who promoted the fiction that Iraqi interpreters had brought the Americans to Iraq which, in turn, led to the assassination of interpreters. This warlord-turned-populist ran on an "Iraq First" campaign very similar to President Donald Trump's. Although only 44.52 percent of voters turned out, his victory indicated the Iraqi peoples' rejection of Western intervention in the country. A comment about the election in the most recent Time magazine summed up the Iraqi attitude: "While the West has been preoccupied with gaining political influence, a real opportunity has been squandered to foster a culture of democracy and respect for human rights. The Iraqi people are now fed up with a lack of progress on addressing poverty, corruption, and the need for essential services."

I could feel the heat of Raad's anger as he hunched over, head in his hands. "You can't imagine what they'll do now. It's the same as putting Al Qaeda and ISIS in the government."

Nisren tried to explain Raad's vehemence. "He always gets so mad when he watches the news," she said. "He doesn't think about anything but Iraq."

Raad's angry words erupted again. He said he had never dreamed about leaving Baghdad or Iraq. Even when he had the opportunity to go to Korea for advanced training in tae kwon do, he refused. "I didn't want to leave when I put my name in for interpreter repatriation in 2003. I just did it in case of the worst. I never, never wanted to leave my country!"

He leaned back on the sofa and took a deep breath. "Don't think I'm not glad to be here. It's a relief to be safe in a great country, people, and tradition, but my heart is over there. Every day I wish I could fly to my county. Some Iraqis I know here go every month, but they weren't interpreters. Worrying about home stops us from living like normal people."

He looked over at me. "I'm sorry," he mumbled.

A minute or two passed in complete silence. I was overwhelmed with a sadness that blocked any response. What could I say anyway? It would be meaningless in the face of the pain Raad felt. His hopes for the homeland he left behind had slipped through his fingers like grains of sand. What could he do when he couldn't leave Iraq behind and couldn't return to the country he had left?

The chirping of the parakeets in the cage broke the silence. Raad again apologized for his anger, excused himself, and went outside.

Part II

Eman

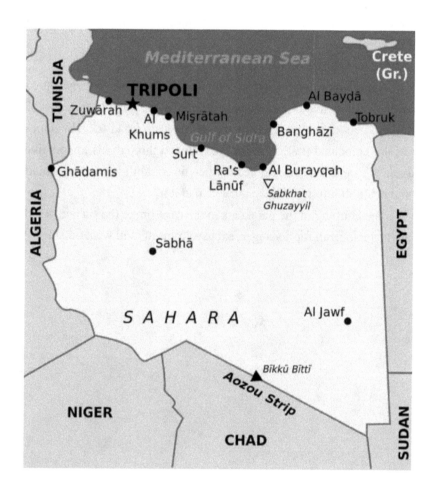

Historical Backdrop: Libya 1983-2016

1983: Eman's birth. Colonel Muammar Qaddafi has been in power for 14 years after deposing King Idris in a military coup.

1984: The United Kingdom (UK) breaks off diplomatic relations with Libya after a British policewoman is shot outside Libyan embassy in London while anti-Qaddafi protests were staged.

1986: The US bombs Libyan military facilities and residential areas of Tripoli and Benghazi, killing more than 100 people, including Qaddafi's adopted daughter. Raids are in response to Libyan bombing of a Berlin disco where there are US military personnel.

1988: A Pan American airliner is blown up over the Scottish town of Lockerbie, allegedly by Libyan agents.

1991: The UN imposes sanctions on Libya in an effort to force the handover for trial of two of its citizens suspected in Lockerbie bombing.

1996: Abu Salim prison massacre: an estimated 1,270 prisoners are slaughtered. Almost all inmates were political prisoners, slated to be interned without trial from 1988 until 2000.

1999: Lockerbie suspects handed over for trial in the Netherlands under Scottish law. UN sanctions suspended and diplomatic relations with the UK restored.

2003: Libya signs a $1.5-billion dollar deal to compensate families of Lockerbie bombing victims. Libya takes responsibility for the bombing in a letter to the UN Security Council. UN Security Council votes to lift sanctions. Libya says it will abandon programs to develop weapons of mass destruction.

2006: The US restores full diplomatic ties with Libya.

2011, February 15: The Day of Revolt. Inspired by Arab Spring revolts in other Arab countries, especially neighboring Egypt and Tunisia, violent protests break out in Benghazi, spread to other cities leading to clashes between security forces and anti-Qaddafi rebels.

March: The UN Security Council authorizes no-fly zone over Libya and air strikes to protect civilians, over which NATO assumes command. Libyan rebels initially capture territory but are then forced back by better-armed pro-Qaddafi forces.

August: Qaddafi goes into hiding after rebels swarm into his fortress compound in Tripoli.

Saif is born.

October: Qaddafi is captured and killed as rebel fighters take his hometown, Sirte. Three days later, the National Transitional Council (NTC) declares Libya to be officially "liberated" and announces plans to hold elections within eight months.

2012, January: Clashes erupt between former rebel forces in Benghazi and the governing NTC, whose deputy head resigns.

March: Tensions arise between NTC officials in the oil-rich east and the central NTC in Tripoli.

June: Government struggles to control local militias, especially in Zintan in the west. The Al-Awfea Brigade briefly takes over Tripoli International Airport.

August: The NTC hands power to the General National Congress (GNC) elected in July.

September: US ambassador and three other Americans are killed when Islamist militants storm the consulate in Benghazi.

2012: Eman and her family arrive in the US

2014: Fighting breaks out between forces loyal to outgoing GNC and new parliament chosen in elections.

UN staff pulls out, embassies are shut down, and foreigners are evaciated as the security situation deteriorates. Tripoli International Airport is largely destroyed by fighting. Ansar Al-Sharia, Islamist terrorists group, seizes control of most of Benghazi.

2015: Sanad is born.

2016: Eman graduates with a Master's of Science in computer science

CHAPTER I

The Sheep Family

THE BABEL OF NEWLY-MINTED ENGLISH SPRINKLED WITH CHINESE, JAPANESE, ARABIC, AND SPANISH SIGNALED LUNCH BREAK FOR THE STUDENTS IN SIX LEVELS OF INSTRUCTION AT SPRING INTERNATIONAL LANGUAGE CENTER ACROSS FROM ARAPAHOE COMMUNITY COLLEGE IN LITTLETON, COLORADO. It was a noise I cherished, but one that might not be compatible with a recorded interview of Libyan student, Eman, in my shared office near the reception desk in the central building. This was Spring's thirty-seventh year in its Littleton location. The 25-hour-a-week ESL program had been through many ups and downs since three couples second-mortgaged our homes in 1979 to start Spring Institute for International Studies in an old Denver public school building in north Denver across from Regis College. From that humble beginning, Spring divided into two separate entities: Spring Institute focusing on a variety of programs for immigrants and refugees, and Spring International Language Center targeting intensive English as a Second Language training for international students. Today, Spring International serves international students in two locations: suburban Littleton and the campus of the University of Arkansas in Fayetteville. Even though I retired as director several years ago, I still maintained an office and kept in touch with my colleagues and the students.

Because I was not teaching when Eman was a student at Spring International, I didn't have the opportunity to know her in the classroom, but I was still able to see the impact she had on her instructors and fellow students. Since she received her Master's of Science diploma from the University of Colorado at Denver in 2016, Eman had been working as a receptionist and computer assistant to fulfill requirements for optional practical training (OPT). Her Arabic language and computer skills, friendliness, and helpfulness had won over students from the more than 15 countries represented in our student body. My request to interview her for a book was met with warmth and excitement. She had a story she was eager to tell.

Most of Eman's time was spent in our annex building just a few doors from the central building where I was waiting for our first interview. I spotted her coming through the double doors with a purposeful stride I soon learned was characteristic of this goal-oriented 32-year-old woman. She was wearing a long tan dress buttoned up the front, a soft brown-and-gold flowered head scarf folded softly around her face and clipped together beneath her chin, and very practical sneakers that would take her to the train and bus that transported her to work four days a week. I realized how similar we were in stature when we greeted each other and touched cheeks, about five foot two, narrow-shouldered, and small-boned, just perfect for a light embrace. Her straight, black eyebrows over expressive hazel eyes were balanced by a wide, ready smile showing perfect white teeth.

We decided to meet in the quiet of a small conference room. It was a comfortable room with a large world map that almost covered the back wall and two framed photos of the Rocky Mountains on the adjoining wall above a computer station. We sat across from each other at the conference table with its ever-present wicker basket half-filled with wrapped peppermint candies. After some conversation about school activities, we were ready to begin her story. I placed my tiny voice recorder on the table between us and fumbled around in my usual technological ineptness to find the appropriate file. Eman asked if she could help, and in a few seconds, she had the recorder cued up and ready to begin.

She laughed as she unfolded a paper of possible questions for our interview. "I did the homework you gave me and thought about my childhood for a long time," she said. She scanned the paper, looked up at the map on the wall, and then sat in silence for a minute.

"I don't know if I should tell you this or not."

"*Zay min awz*, as you wish," I said.

She leaned across the table and whispered, "I really didn't like my childhood."

As our interview progressed, I learned that Eman was born in 1983 in the village of Al Khadra, a suburb of Tarhuna, a city in the northwestern part of Libya named after a Berber tribe of pre-Roman era inhabitants. Tarhuna is about two hours on a two-lane road from Tripoli, the capital city of 1.1 million people and the residence of the Guide, or Leader, as Muammar Qaddafi demanded to be called. Eman is a Sunni Muslim, as is ninety-seven percent of the population of Libya, which numbers only seven million people. The overwhelming homogeneity of religion stands in contrast to Nisren's Iraq where approximately sixty-five percent of the population is Shiite Muslim; fifteen to twenty percent, Arab Sunni Muslim; and seventeen percent Sunni Kurdish Muslim, a more secular group.

Eman was born into a family of four siblings from her father's first wife. Ten years after her birth, her father married a second wife, so by the time she was sixteen, her total family numbered 23 children, including Eman. When her father was born after Libya's independence in 1951, the economy was based mainly on field and tree crops and livestock products. It was a hard life with only sparse stretches of productive land, no rivers, and limited rainfall and groundwater. This was a time when farmers who lived off their harvest and their livestock couldn't afford to pay extra laborers and could only depend on themselves and their children. A large family might be their only assurance of survival. Multiple wives produced more children, so polygyny was common.

I shook my head in amazement. "A family of twenty-three siblings and two mothers?"

Eman smiled. "This doesn't make sense to you, does it?

"I do understand this," I said thinking back to my Egyptian experience, "especially in a time when Libya was just developing. Just living day to day was a priority. I would guess that lack of education was a factor too." Eman agreed and noted that education and progress have impacted Libyan marriage and family patterns. She was quick to point out that marrying multiple wives is legal in Libya today, but very few men practice it. Statistics supported that view with only 2.57 percent of marriages reported as polygynous during Libya's last census in 2006 coupled with an average household size of only five persons. This is a remarkable difference in family structure between Eman's and her parents' generations.

"My religion allows a man to have four wives but only if he can treat them equally and justly. This is very difficult," she nodded. "but Muhammad, peace be upon him, made big differences in a woman's rights and her role in marriage."

My favorite religious historian, Houston Smith, explains the honor and status that Muhammad brought to women in an age, the last half of the sixth century AD, when women were considered of little worth. "Marriage arrangements were so loose as to be hardly recognizable. . . Women were regarded as little more than chattel, to be done with as fathers or husbands pleased. Daughters had no inheritance rights and were often buried alive in their infancy." According to the Koran, the Islamic holy book, marriage was the only lawful place for the sexual act. It also stated that a woman must give her free consent before she could be married, and finally, it tightened the marriage bond by making divorce only a last resort.

Today, this practice, in addition to cultural influences, supports the relatively low divorce to marriage ratio of twenty-three percent in Libya while the US Census Bureau reports this same ratio in the United States is forty-six percent, double that of Libya.

Statistics aside, how did more than two dozen children, two wives, and one husband actually function as a family? In second marriages in the US, it is difficult enough to bring children and stepchildren together as a unit but, if you added both the mother and the step-mother to the household, it would be a prescription for disaster. I learned the possible secret of success in such a situation as my interviews with Eman progressed. Only the qualities of patience, understanding, and tolerance she exhibited could amicably smooth the way for two complete families living together. However, it was still difficult for me to fathom how she could flourish and achieve in competition with so many siblings.

How could a father and mother pay attention to and encourage each child? Would there be enough food for all the children? As an only child, I couldn't envision what daily life would be like surrounded by so many siblings. Would I have been able to find a quiet corner to read a book? What about the privacy of my own bedroom? Would I have any one-on-one time with my mom and dad? One benefit did occur to me. I wouldn't have had the burden of being the sole focus of my mother's life in such a family. I didn't have time to voice these thoughts because Eman was eagerly forging ahead with her story.

She straightened her shoulders and leaned back in her chair. She wanted me to truly understand the reality of her situation. "In spite of the size of the family, my mom still took good care of each of us and encouraged us to be the best we could be. My mom worked so hard in the house. We had to get water from a well outside the kitchen, fill a big container, and hand it to one of the kids inside who would take it to the kitchen and the bathrooms," she explained. "We didn't even have a washing machine until I was about 21 when my sister and I earned money and bought one. Before that, mama had to get up early to heat water on the kitchen stove to wash our clothes. Of course, our house had electricity, but sometimes in the winter when there was rain and wind, the power lines would break, and we'd have to use candles at night."

Her mother was married when she was in her twenties and bore eleven living children during the next 20 years. Sometimes there were only one to two years between pregnancies. "My mother had twin girls, but they passed away," she said. "When she had me, she was in the hospital with my aunt who was having a baby at the same time. A tumor in my mom's breast had to be removed, so I only nursed three days from her milk and then my aunt took care of me with formula." In spite of the many pregnancies, her mother, who is now in her 60s, is healthy but "very, very thin."

This large, active family required an equally large, sprawling house. Her father, she proudly told me, had constructed their house of cement block on one level with numerous additions to accommodate the growing family. She took her pen and sketched the house on her notepad, so I could better visualize it. In its finished state, the structure had an open-to-the sky passage way connecting two wings, one for each wife and her children, with an open court yard in the middle. Each wife had a separate kitchen and bedroom of her own. The girls from each family had a shared bedroom in each wing and the same for the boys. The children slept on mattresses that were laid out on the floor each evening. Overnight visitors slept in a guest bedroom. There were three bathrooms, one in Eman's wing and two in her half-siblings' section, which were busily used to get ready for school and to do ablutions before prayers. Later when an adult child married and wanted to stay with the family, another bedroom would be added on top of the original structure. On her only visit home since she arrived in the US, she had jokingly rejected her dad's idea of enclosing the long passageway to make more rooms. "The house is like a school building, so we need the open space for the family to line up before classes," she advised her father.

The family house didn't expand for a second wife until ten years after Eman was born, and the strong relationship with her father had already formed. Her grandmother had ordered her father to marry a second wife so there would be more children to care for the sheep and goats she owned and which contributed to the livelihood of the entire family. Her father, with the respect required of a son, married again, and his new wife bore an additional twelve children.

I shook my head in amazement and sympathy for those two mothers who endured an endless routine of pregnancies and childbirths, especially considering they had no means or choice to say "No, thank you. This is enough."

If the women were asked about their childbearing, would they say it was Allah's will to have so many children?"

"Yes," she nodded, "they believed their reward for giving birth and serving as good mothers would come in heaven."

I knew how much Eman missed her mother and loved her. I thought about the drain on my own patience in caring for two daughters just seventeen months apart and a few years later adding an active little boy to the mix. How would a mother keep her sanity with so many children to care for? Wouldn't they continually be quarreling and vying for attention?

Eman paused, looked up at the mountain scene on the wall, and breathed deeply. She seemed to be seeing her distant mother in her mind. "I learned the meaning of patience from my mother. She taught me how to keep going no matter what was happening. From her, I learned how to work really hard to reach goals and to keep trying no matter what. When I look back, I realize that growing up in a big family taught me to share my feelings, my possessions, and the responsibilities of the household. When I was little, we couldn't afford to buy a basket full of fruit, but we always shared a few apples and bananas. We would cut the apples into slices and share them with each other. We felt so happy because all of us got to try a little. As we grew up, we had some good times together with both families, drinking tea, having fun, and making jokes, but as children, it was difficult to know each other well because we had so little time to speak in depth."

Besides lack of time, there was only enough money for their basic needs. "My father worked extra hard to earn money, so he could support us and our education. He would buy us all school supplies and check to make sure we had everything we needed for school.

Religious and custom-related rules governed both children and adults. Eman's strong Sunni beliefs provided the framework for her life, much more so than Nisren's more secular viewpoint. Belief in Allah was the most important element in her world view. In first and second grade, Libyan students begin to study the Koran, which is the literal focus of God's words. Even before formal study, Eman had learned and observed the Five Pillars of Islam, which are the guideposts of Muslim life: the testimony of faith, five prayers a day, fasting during the month of Ramadan, giving support to the needy fasting during Ramadan, and the pilgrimage to Mecca. Her mother had taught her to say the testimony of faith: "There is no true god but God (Allah) and Muhammad is the Messenger (prophet) of God." She believed, as most Muslims, in the existence of angels as honored creatures who worshipped God, obeyed Him, and acted only by His command. Gabriel was the angel who brought the words of the Koran down to Muhammad.

"As a child, I had the image of two angels, one counting good deeds and the other, bad deeds," Eman explained. "I knew that when you ask Allah, ma sh'allah, glorified and exalted be He, to forgive you, the bad deed will be erased." She explained her vision of Allah with a scale that weighs good and bad deeds, and whichever is the heavier determines paradise or hell. As a child, she believed that angels were an inner voice that talked to her. "I always wanted to be a good Muslim and a good girl, which meant I had to respect older people, obey my mother and father, pray five times a day, and not make friendships with boys, not be seen with them. I could say 'Hi' and 'Bye' with boy cousins but not talk personally with them."

I stopped for a minute to take a drink of bottled water and to look behind me at the large map of the world. Libya, and its strong religious and family culture, stretched an arm's length from one side of the map to where we were today in the middle of the United States. The physical distance between the two countries was made even longer by the cultural and religious differences in our life experiences. Our hands met as we both reached for a peppermint candy from the basket on the conference table. We laughed at our shared need for something sweet. Eman asked me if she was talking too much. I told her that I was fascinated by every detail and understood why such a large family made her childhood so difficult.

She shook her head. "Oh, no, that's not why I didn't like my childhood. My big family had nothing to do with that. The worst thing was my grandmother's sheep."

"Sheep? Why sheep?" I asked.

A typical day with the sheep, reconstructed from Eman's description, explained her negative attitude.

It was eight-year-old Eman's turn to watch the sheep. Her grandmother, Amna, had paired her up with Susu, her first cousin, because she knew the children would pay more attention to the flock if they weren't close siblings who wanted to play rather than work, The sheep were the most important part of her grandmother's life and livelihood, but they were a pain to her grandchildren, whose daily lives were scheduled around their noon to sunset care. "Mama, why can't Baba just tell grandmother that we've had enough?" she would complain. "No more sheep. We want to watch cartoons." Her mother would explain that it was important for their father to show respect to his mother by doing as she asked.

"Just be patient," she said. "You are doing a good deed each time you work with the sheep. What you're asking for will come eventually. Remember that Allah will recognize those good deeds."

It was almost noon when Eman skipped through the entrance to their wing of the house and almost time for mid-day prayers. Four of her sisters were in the bedroom they shared, laughing and talking about their school day. Eman didn't have time to join them because she needed to change quickly from her blue school uniform into sandals and an old dress that reached her ankles. She had folded up yesterday's dress and put it aside because it was dirty and had a tear in the back where "that evil ram" had butted her with his long curled horns. She remembered falling down and playing dead, looking up from the corner of one eye to see if the ram would go away. After a few minutes, he left, and she could get up. Every time she changed clothes, she made a wish for a pretty new dress rather than wearing something recycled through the girls in the family. A small green and blue scarf covered her curly black hair and framed her heart-shaped face and wide honey-brown eyes. She had recently decided for herself that she would wear hijab although most girls waited until they were 10 or 11 to cover their hair.

Eman hurried to the kitchen to ask her mother, Khadeja, for some tea and a sandwich to take with her to the sheep farm. In a pink-flowered wrap-around cloak with a hood in the back that pulled up to partially cover her hair, her mother was stirring a pot of couscous on the wood-burning stove, one of many chores that had added deep lines to her once-pretty face. A tattoo ran vertically from her lower lip to her chin, a centuries-old tradition in North Africa and the Middle East denoting beauty and protection from evil. She paused to pat Eman on her shoulder and said, "Eziak, habibti?" Her "How are you, sweetheart?" brought a loving hug from her daughter. Mama was always cheerful in spite of the difficult childhood she had suffered, having to leave her own mother to begin living with her father's new wife after he had divorced her mom. It was made even more difficult for her when her husband took an additional wife. She wasn't happy, but she firmly believed that Allah would grant her many good deeds for her labor and sacrifice. If not in her lifetime, she would be rewarded on Judgment Day. As the two sets of children grew up, they became friends and joined together as one family.

Eman poured some tea into a jam jar, made a quick sandwich and grabbed one of her fourth-grade school books and a small radio as she ran into the courtyard to meet her cousin Susu for the twenty-five minute walk to her grandmother's nearest farm just a few miles from Al Khadra. Eman wanted to hurry to the farm to get the unwelcome task over with, but Susu lagged behind kicking rocks along the dirt path.

As they walked over a small hill near the house of a relative, they could hear the distant baa-ing of the fat-tailed Barbary sheep and the softer maa-ing of their spring lambs. Susu reached out, tugged on the edge of Eman's dress, and shouted, "Watch out for that mean dog,"

The grouchy old man and his mongrel dog usually sat outside the house keeping watch for the children on their way to the farm and on the way back with their sheep. He always put out a large dish of food for the dog and didn't want the sheep near it. The girls were suspicious of his reason for putting out the food when he knew they were coming down the path. They knew he didn't want the passel of kids from their family or their sheep anywhere near his house. Just as they approached his property, a skinny, gray dog dashed out from under an olive tree, growling and baring his teeth at the pair. Susu and Eman started running down the path, and the dog took off after them. Susu's long legs propelled her twenty feet ahead of Eman, who had lost one of her sandals as she ran.

"Don't stop now. He'll get you," Susu yelled over her shoulder. When the dog came to the edge of its property, it stopped and stood guard, growling at the kids as they faded into the distance.

When they arrived at the farm, just one of the five that grandmother owned, Eman leaned against an almond tree and rubbed the bottom of her sore foot. "Maybe I can find my shoe when we herd the sheep back down the path."

Grazing intently on green scrub and grass were 40 or 50 sandy-brown colored sheep. Both sexes were adorned with large horns that swept backwards and outwards in an arch, looking like a cross between a goat and a sheep. A few rogues were wandering off into property that didn't belong to the family. There were no fences, but the girls knew which trees and rocks marked their land. Susu grabbed a strong olive branch she had left under a tree the last time she was scheduled to watch the sheep. "Shush! Shush!" she shouted as she ran around the perimeter of the flock, waving the branch like a lariat to scare the stray sheep back into the flock.

In an attempt to give each other time out from their task, the girls took turns herding the sheep. Susu was first, so Eman was free to put down the things she had brought under the shade of her favorite olive tree. It was a century-old tree with a gnarled and twisted gray trunk full of bumps and cracks, but even at this age, it could still celebrate spring with some small white flowers in loose clusters. Other olive trees were in full blossom along with a few almond trees which spread a honeyed scent that mixed with the lanolin sheep smell in the warm afternoon air.

She sat down, tuned in some music on the battery-operated radio, and picked up her arithmetic book to do her homework. Books, homework, school, and learning, in general, were the favorite parts of her life. Tending sheep was her least favorite. No family in Al Khadra was as large as Eman's, and no other family required daily care of sheep. It didn't help that her classmates and the neighbors frequently taunted her and her siblings by shouting "There goes the sheep family." As she tired of the bullying, she learned to respond with "We have to care for sheep, but look who gets the good grades." A girlfriend jokingly told her that she'd like to be one of the sheep because she would get more care and attention than she did at home.

Eman kept looking up from her book, hoping that her aging grandmother wouldn't visit the farm that day, find her loafing under the tree, and scold her for not paying attention to her job. The two little girls took turns shouting and herding the straying sheep back into the flock until dusk when they could herd the sheep into a pen and then return to the house. She walked barefoot with her one remaining sandal in her hand but never found its match.

Compiling Eman's descriptions of her most-hated childhood task heightened my appreciation of her adult achievements. From sheepherding to a master's degree in computer science was a giant leap. I wondered if there was a bit of her powerful grandmother in Eman. I encouraged her to tell me more about this woman named Amna.

With respect in her voice and a spark of humor in her eyes, she described her grandmother as an entrepreneur in a time when women did not head a family and certainly did not own and operate a business. In the 1950s when her two sons and three daughters were still young, her husband, a brother, and cousin died in a tragic automobile accident. A Romanian truck crashed into their vehicle on the way to Benghazi. This loss of three family members at the same time could have devastated Amna, but she knew that she had to care for her children. She had no choice but to become the independent head of the family. This was difficult, but she was well-trained as the only daughter in a family of sons. Her father had treated her like a boy, teaching her to ride horses, shoot a rifle, plant a wheat crop, and raise sheep. The sheep and a small herd of goats were her only way to survive. In an unheard-of task for a woman, she approached local government officials and convinced them to sell her several farms that had been established after Italy had occupied Libya. "She was a unique woman for her generation," Eman said. "Her life also showed the changes in Libya over the years from living in a big tent with her growing family to moving to a house built of metal and finally to a concrete home that my dad built." Her grandmother's favorite saying was Eman's legacy: "Swallow it now, and you will taste the sweetness later."

I was beginning to understand the power that Amna had over her son. The family story of his infancy was legendary. He had been a handsome baby with white skin and curly black hair. Evidently, a mean woman who was a visitor to the house looked at the baby, admired him, and predicted that he would not live until the next day; in other words, she cast "the evil eye" on the baby, a curse believed in many cultures to cause illness or injury with just a malevolent glare. Within twenty-four hours, the baby's left eye had become infected and soon after he was completely blind in that eye. As he grew up, his mother ruled his life with an iron fist. Because he wanted to honor her, he obeyed her every command, including the ruling that his numerous children had to tend the sheep. Serving one's parents, in Islam, is a duty second only to prayer, and expressing irritation at parental demands is considered despicable. Eman's father was bound by this commandment. In American society, however, obedience to parents is a loose thread that is tugged on by our culture's stress on independence and individuality. Talking back to mom and dad, challenging family rules, and choosing to go your own way are common responses to parents who demand obedience. In turn, parents' reactions are often diluted into a weak mixture of "Because I said so" or "Watch it, or you'll be grounded." As Eman told her story, I could see the concept of honoring parents was woven into her character. It strengthened the ties that bound her to her family and added to her homesickness in America.

Eman and I left the sheep story behind because the noise of students returning to their afternoon classes signaled her required return to the reception desk in the other building. Before turning off the recorder, I had one last question:

"How old were you when you stopped taking care of the sheep?"

"I was twenty-three," she responded.

CHAPTER 2

Growing Up with Qaddafi

BY THE TIME OF EMAN'S BIRTH IN 1983, THE DICTATOR MUAMMAR QADDAFI HAD ALREADY CONTROLLED LIBYA WITH A STRONG FIST FOR FOURTEEN YEARS. In spite of his eccentricity, he was destined to become the Arab world's longest reigning dictator. A many-faceted personality cult had developed around Colonel Qaddafi from the time he and his fellow military plotters had overthrown Libya's King Idris in 1969. His face adorned murals, posters, and postage stamps and his Green Book became a sacred treatise forced into the memories of the people. But for the child Eman, Qaddafi was just the wallpaper and the background noise of everyday life. School took center stage.

"I loved to learn and was so happy in school," Eman said. Her rose and blue hijab and positive energy lit up the small windowless class room we were meeting in this afternoon. She had pulled two student armchair desks together for our interview. Two of the walls were covered with large sheets of paper listing parts of the human anatomy, the topic of the week for a class of Japanese nurses. When the group of five nineteen-year-olds had been welcomed by Eman at orientation, she told them she had been studying English at Spring not too long ago and knew they would succeed in their language goals just as she had. The young women had never before met a Muslim, let alone a Libyan, so they asked for a special class hour to ask questions and learn more about her country.

My mind retreated to 1977 when I met my first Libyan student. I was teaching ESL and initiating a homestay program at Bridge International Language Center on the Denver campus of Colorado Women's College. We received a group of young Libyan men with scholarships directly from Qaddafi, all of whom were to major in a field that their government called "atomic engineering." They were intelligent and well mannered, and most of them were not at all interested in atomic engineering nor in returning to Libya. In the 1970s, Qaddafi had many accomplishments to his credit: providing scholarships for university degrees in the US and England, free public education with primary school compulsory for both sexes, free health care, and the introduction of laws giving more power to women. He legally affirmed equality of the sexes and wage parity in addition to supporting a law that criminalized marriage of females under the age of sixteen and affirmed that a woman's consent was a prerequisite for marriage. Along with the benefits came increased political repression. The year the students came to Denver marked the beginning of revolutionary committees that were used to survey the population in Libya and repress any political opposition to Qaddafi's autocratic rule. Reportedly, ten to twenty percent of Libyans worked as spies for these committees. These "eyes on us" informants were on a par with Saddam Hussein's Ba'athist regime in Iraq. Each group of students had its own informants who were ordered to spy on the students and report missteps to the government at home. When my husband and I were invited to a dinner with all the Libyan students in the Denver area, our Libyan students pointed out the spies in the group who were taking photos of students talking to their American guests. Spying aside, all but two of the group completed university degrees — and in some cases, advanced studies — and managed to remain in the United States.

The 2011 revolution in Libya, followed by the failure of the state, freed Eman from the "spying eyes" that haunted students of the 70s and 80s. She was free to befriend and encourage Spring International's students in language learning. It was a joy that grew from her parents' respect for education. Neither Eman's father nor her mother had the opportunity to go to school, but they valued education for all of their children. Baba would buy school supplies for each child at the beginning of the school year and celebrate their good grades with cake for all the students in the class. When the girls in the family were fourteen or fifteen years old, their mom would give them a schedule of household tasks, but when they had exams, studies were more important, and she would excuse them from work. Grandmother wasn't just interested in the welfare of her flocks of sheep; she also showed pride in her grandkids' progress in school. "We would show our good grades to her, and she would reward us with treats. Then she could brag and tell her friends and family about her smart grandchildren," Eman remembered.

Eman and her many siblings were beneficiaries of Qaddafi's educational reforms but also unknowing victims of the political repression. There were no knocks on the door from secret police, no exposure to kidnapping, hangings, or other violence. She was as sheltered as the sheep she herded but fenced in with the invisible barriers of culture and religion. Even as a small child, she had a clear focus on learning that blurred all outside turmoil. As we discussed her school years, she told me about a lucky incident that propelled her into first grade when she was just five years old. Her seven-year-old cousin Faraj adored her and always wanted to be with her. When it came time for him to start school, he refused to go.

"I want Eman to go with me," he demanded.

Neither his father nor his mother could convince him to begin school on the first day with his siblings. He cried and cried and asked for his favorite cousin. The only solution was for Faraj's father to ask five-year-old Eman to accompany him, so she could comfort him and help him with his lessons. She had been counting the months until she was old enough to begin school, so she jumped at the chance to be a companion to Faraj in first grade. She sat next to him to encourage and help him understand the teacher. She also impressed the teachers with her intelligence and quick learning ability, so she became part of the class as a regular student. She remained in the same classes with Faraj until she completed elementary school when he fell behind and had to repeat classes.

A typical school day began about 7 a.m. with all the children seven years old and up jostling each other for bathroom time, eating a bite of breakfast, putting on their school uniforms, and hurrying outside the rambling house.

"*Ta a'la, Ta a'la*," Baba shouted. "Hurry up! Hurry up! It's time to get in the truck. Time for school." Like soldiers getting ready for a maneuver, eight children from Eman's immediate family and her uncle's kids—all of them too little to walk the three miles to primary school— boarded the old, dented construction truck. Their father helped the little girls up first, so they could sit toward the front avoiding the wheelbarrow in one corner and perching on the space over the wheels. They were all dressed in their clean blue uniforms, boys with pants and shirts and girls in long dresses.

Eman got in front with Baba because she was in seventh grade then, so it would be haram, shameful, to sit in back with the boys. Two of her girl cousins who were bigger were already in the front seat, so Eman had to prop herself up on one of their laps grasping her school books and the special paper she had prepared the night before. Baba adjusted the small, white knit cap on his head, smoothed his long, white shirt over his trousers, and squeezed in the front seat beside the girls.

It took the truck less than thirty minutes to reach Al Khadra, a small village within Tarhuna City. As the vehicle bumped along the dirt road, the children could glimpse remaining bits of Libya's revolving-door history. No relics were left behind by the original Berber population or by the Carthaginians, Phoenicians, and Greeks that followed from 700 to 400 BC. But very visible to the children and to tourists were pieces of Roman columns and statues from as far back as 74 BC. As the truck neared the school, it passed an ancient mosque that was a reminder of the Arab conquest of Libya in 643 AD and the beginning of Islam. Other Turkish-style mosques in the area were remnants of the Ottoman Empire's conquest of Libya in 1551. A large migration of Turks dominated political and social life of the region, which, as a result of intermarriage, changed the ethnic mix of the country. The children in Baba's truck were more excited about getting close to school than they were about the scenery on the way. Eman knew that the old building that housed her prep school was built by the Italians. Her study of Libya's history acknowledged that it was a reminder of one of the most violent campaigns in the history of colonialism. Italy invaded the country after a brief war with the Ottomans in 1912. The Libyans fought back until a truce was brokered by the British after Italy joined the Allies in World War I. After the war, fighting broke out again as Italy continued efforts to colonize Libya. Mussolini used brutal tactics, including an air campaign of bombing and poison gas, to finally seize control of the coastal cities, unifying Tripolitania and Cyrenaica as the colony of Libya in 1929. In 1943, when the Italian-German armies were defeated in North Africa, Libya fell to the British and the French, who governed it until independence in 1951 when they appointed Muhammed Idris Al-Sanusi, a Libyan religious and political leader, as king. The children studied this history of invasion after invasion, but what they knew first-hand was the final chapter: In

1969, Colonel Muammar Al-Qaddafi staged a military coup deposing King Idris and was recognized as their Leader, their Guide and, to many followers, a hero who could do no wrong.

It would be almost 8:30 when the truck with all the children arrived at the three buildings that comprised the school campus. The younger children piled out of the truck bed and ran to form lines outside the primary school. Eman, nervously holding the special paper she had written, and her two older cousins queued up next door in front of the old building that served preparatory school students. A third newer building on the same school grounds was occupied by the high school. All three buildings had two floors with classrooms filled with boys and girls in separate rows.

A boy in second grade rang the bell in the courtyard, and the morning ritual began. Five minutes of exercises came first, led by a teacher who then directed the students in singing the Libyan national anthem while another student raised Libya's solid green flag up the flag pole, the only national flag in the world with just one color and no design. Voices from soprano first-graders to baritone twelfth graders melded together to sing: "All colors have meaning, but green has special meaning as the color of paradise, the symbol of life and prosperity. The green flag is calling, asking Allah for help to defeat its enemies with faith and with weapons. I will fight for my country and the light of right is bright on my hands."

Then it was Eman's turn to be in the spotlight. She walked to the front of the line and stood next to the teacher. Carefully unfolding the paper she had written the night before, she read: "Word of the Day: Honesty." In a loud, clear voice, she defined the word and explained its application to school work and everyday life.

In addition to frequently being chosen to read the "Word of the Day," Eman had perfected her Arabic calligraphy to the point that teachers and even people outside the school asked her to print reports, signs, posters, and advertising for them. This would have been a compliment until she discovered that most of these people were claiming her calligraphy as their own work. "They never gave me credit nor mentioned my name. You get paid for being a teacher, but I got nothing," she commented later. "Unfortunately, in Libyan culture you must try to please others and not say 'No' to numerous requests for help."

After the morning ritual was accomplished, the students hurried to their grade-level classrooms where they would sit on separate benches, boys on one side and girls on the other. They passed under the eyes of Leader and Guide Qaddafi, whose large portraits were displayed in the hallways and administration offices. Also displayed prominently were quotes from his *Green Book*, a 21,000-word manifesto that combined utopian socialism, Arab nationalism, and everything from the importance of owning a car to the evils of mechanized poultry farming. Study of *The Green Book* was mandated from fourth grade through high school. "We were tested on its contents," she explained. "It was very, very important, but you know what, honestly, it was mainly just words, something written."

Among the many somewhat meaningless sentences, there also were rules about good behavior, responsibility in school, and more than 60 dates in Libyan history that students had to memorize. "The book was honored, just as our green flag was, and no one could do bad things to either one, or they would be reported." She told me about a friend who took the flag and tied it on a tree branch, which was considered an insult, so she was reported to the government. Her punishment was not known.

Public schools were part of Libya's form of statehood, the *Jamahiriya*, an Arabic term generally translated as "state of the masses" or "people's republic." More than half the Libyan population was on the government payroll. It was almost impossible to exist outside of the *Jamahiriya* because almost everyone was connected to it somehow, for housing or for their jobs. What this meant was that many Libyans' primary loyalty lay not to the state but to their tribe, their ethnic group. Stay on Qaddafi's good side, and your tribe might be given control of a ministry or a good business concession; fall on his bad side, and you're all out in the cold.

Eman remembered thinking, "We should have someone working in the army, and then we would have more money." Her father was working in his own construction business, but one of her uncles was in Qaddafi's military, so he had cars, and his daughters always had new dresses for Muslim holidays, like Eid al-fitr, which celebrated the end of Ramadan. Qaddafi didn't have to worry about divisions on religious lines—virtually all Libyan citizens were Sunni Muslims—but he did need to think about drawing into his ruling circle the requisite number of people from the two major cities on the Mediterranean coast, Misurata and Benghazi, to keep everyone mollified. If that didn't work, then the Mukhabarat, the secret police, would round up enemies of the state, real or imagined. These people were thrown into prison after sham trials or simply executed on the spot. Education came under the purview of the Jamahiriya. Every year, a meeting would be scheduled in each city to decide the needs of each school. Reports were written and then the committee would discuss all the requests and vote about decisions. These decisions would be announced, but usually needs such as infrastructure and expansion of the faculty were not addressed, and the same issues came up every year, according to Eman.

As a seventh grader, Eman gained confidence even though she was the youngest student in the class. When she was in primary school, children would occasionally tease her about being part of "the sheep family" or ask her why she was wearing hijab when she was only in the second half of 1st grade.

"In the beginning, it was hard because they laughed and made jokes and tried to pull the scarf off my head." She endured the bullying but continued firmly in her decision to cover her hair. The strict rules of behavior in all levels of public education in Libya pressured her to be quiet and obedient. In preparatory school, the equivalent of American middle school, she frequently stayed in her seat during breaks between classes while the students rushed outdoors.

Observing the physical punishment for misbehavior was a good reason to follow the rules. "When the teacher wanted to punish us for talking too much," Eman explained, "she would make girls sit next to boys, so we would be silent the whole time." Other punishments were delivered by hitting students' hands with a stick if they were late, striking them on the bottom of their bare feet if they received bad grades, or making them stand on one foot with their hands in the air for an entire class period. The rigid instruction and physical punishment were discouraging to some of her siblings. "One of my brothers hated school and left at ninth grade," she said. "Another brother in fourth or fifth grade would ride in the truck to school with us, get out, and run back home. My mom would convince him to go back, and the teacher would punish him publicly by making him write all his numbers on the board in descending order."

When Eman reached high school, she blossomed into an outgoing, talkative young lady. She and her half-sister, Koko, became very close. "Other kids at school would say, 'Aren't you sisters? Why are you always together? Haven't you finished talking yet?'" They even wore the same outfits sometimes just to make people comment. They would talk at home until 2 a.m. and laugh until they cried. The only task that interrupted their conversation was the nightly assignment for Eman to go to her aging grandmother's house to watch over her, so someone would be there if she got up and was disoriented. "The next day, I would finish my conversation with Koko."

English language instruction in public schools depended on the whim of Qaddafi, based on whether or not the United Kingdom and the United States were on his good side. Eman was lucky because she began learning the English alphabet, some reading and grammar, and formation of questions in seventh grade. When her future husband Sami was in school, several years earlier, Qaddafi had dropped English from the curriculum as part of his campaign in 1986 to "eliminate foreign influence." English and French textbooks at Tripoli University were burned by university officials in spite of student protests. For a decade following the book-burning, teaching of French and English was banned in Libya.

When she went to tend the sheep with her cousin, she would use the English words she knew and those her cousin had memorized to make up sentences. When other people heard her speak some English, they were amazed because speaking the language was a nightmare for most Libyans and many repeated high school because of low English scores. "When we had English exams, the students in my class would go early to save me a seat in the middle so they could try to look at my test paper."

Eman's entrepreneurial skills also began at this time. She would take wool from old clothes and knit scarves to sell at school or to relatives, and then with that money, she would buy yarn. Sometimes she would even knit while herding sheep until one day when she lost a big needle at one of the farms, metaphorically a needle in a haystack, but actually a needle in the olive orchard. With the money she earned, she was finally able to buy the pretty dress she had wished for since she was a little girl.

Her days were packed with as many tasks as her house was crowded with children. Studying, housekeeping, caring for her elderly grandmother, and sheepherding occupied almost every minute of Eman's life. The fluctuations of Qaddafi's leadership and the dangers that existed in Libya were in the background but not outwardly spoken about.

"During my childhood years, I always thought of Libya as a safe country," she said. "Qaddafi was a superstar. He was our Leader, our Guide. We couldn't ask questions because we wouldn't get answers if we did. Everything was hidden, private. We knew there were groups against Qaddafi, but we didn't talk about that because of his spies. We did know that our Leader didn't like people who looked like revolutionaries, close to Allah, such as women who were completely veiled and men with beards and Muslim dress. He thought they were hiding their bad deeds in the name of Islam." Whether it was Saddam Hussein in Iraq or Muammar Qaddafi in Libya, dictators in general feared that religious worshippers might plot against them during activities where groups of believers joined together. In Libya, Qaddafi was against these people and would put them in jail. One of Eman's relatives who taught the Koran had five sons who followed strict Muslim laws. They were put in jail for many years, released, and jailed again. They had done nothing wrong.

Even though Eman remained mostly unaware of dangerous happenings in the country, she did remember hearing the noise of bombs falling in Tripoli at the same time that her mother was having a baby at home. US President Ronald Reagan had ordered major bombing raids against Tripoli and Benghazi in 1986, killing forty-five Libyan military and government personnel as well as fifteen civilians; allegedly among them was Qaddafi's adopted baby daughter. This retaliatory strike followed US interception of messages from Libya's East Berlin embassy suggesting that Qaddafi had been involved in a bomb explosion in West Berlin's discotheque nightclub frequented by US servicemen. Then in 1988, when Eman was five, the Lockerbie bombing made world headlines. Libyan agents blew up a Pan Am airliner over the Scottish town of Lockerbie, killing all aboard. In the four years that followed, the UN imposed sanctions on Libya in an effort to force it to hand over for trial two of the Libyans suspected of involvement in the bombing of the airliner. It wasn't until 1999 that Qaddafi handed over the Lockerbie suspects, and UN sanctions were lifted.

When I told Eman that these events made headlines in US newspapers, she had only a vague knowledge of them. Although black and white television was available in Libya in 1968, her family did not own a set. Newspapers were not available in her home as she was growing up, and even if both forms of communication had been available, they were state-owned and not free to print anything other than Qaddafi's version of the truth. Many similarities occurred to me when comparing Eman and Nisren's stories of life in dictatorships: suppression of freedom of speech by imprisonment or death; neighborhood block watches; requirements of residents to inform them of anti-dictatorship activity; an "ideology," like Qaddafi's Green Book, that citizens are never permitted to question; and the ability of the dictator to make war or commit mass murders at a whim. Narcissism was a trait both of these men shared, a characteristic marked by a greatly exaggerated sense of their own importance, preoccupation with their own achievements, constant demands for admiration, and lack of empathy for the feelings and needs of others.

In 1996, when Eman was 13, she heard rumors about killings at Abu Salim, a prison 89 kilometers from her home. In the Abu Salim prison massacre, an estimated 1,270 prisoners were slaughtered over two days. Almost all Abu Salim inmates were political prisoners, slated to be interned without trial from 1988 until 2001 on "political charges." They were herded from their cells into five locked courtyards. Machine-gun bullets rained down from a high tower while khaki-uniformed soldiers wearing green bandannas ran along the flat roofs above the yards, shooting at the trapped men with AK-47s. Other soldiers shot at them from ground level, and those who were not dead at this point were finished off with single shots from automatic pistols. The Abu Salim incident was the trigger that started the chain of events that ultimately led to the overthrow of Qaddafi.

The determination to achieve her goals of advanced education and self-sufficiency provided normality for Eman no matter what happened in the Qaddafi regime or her huge, extended family. However, the rituals of daily life locked her up in a social prison that required hours of her time. Engagements, weddings, births, and deaths were priorities. Any empty spots on her calendar were filled with work toward her goal of higher education. "I would pray to Allah to help me achieve my dreams, to guide me in my decisions. In Islam, we do not just ask for things; we realize that Allah wants us to work for them," she explained. As Eman related the goals and challenges of her story, I realized that these were always accepted with a deep sense of the presence of Allah in her life.

After graduation from high school, she studied for three years at the Higher Institute for Professional Studies where she received a professional diploma in 2003. The Institute was just one of a significant number of universities and institutions in Libya that served the population of only seven million. Libya's first university was established in the 1950s, and at the time of Eman's studies, there were 13 state universities and seven private universities. In addition, the technical sector administered an additional ninety-one institutes with a combined enrollment of 71,000 students, *World Education News and Reviews* reported in 2013.

Eman's Institute diploma enabled her to start working at an internet café, a job that was unusual for a woman because she would be interacting with both sexes. Her knowledge of the computer helped her to train customers to use MS Word in addition to the duties of brewing and serving coffee and tea. The café owner took advantage of her by not paying her regularly and not as much as promised. In order to earn additional money, she and her sister, Dee Dee, began a home business. With money from their outside work, they bought their own computer, a dream of Eman's since she had first glimpsed the technology in middle school. Many hours of paid work were necessary to purchase the computer, which cost about five months of her salary, when and if it were paid. With the new computer, the sisters began typing papers for university students by connecting with an office supply store that offered their typing services. Because her sister owned a cell phone, the store would inform her when a paper was ready to be picked up and typed.

Eman's brother Wesam encouraged her to leave the internet café and apply for a government job because she would be paid more and, hopefully on a regular basis. She found a teaching job with the Ministry of Higher Education to work in a small school with only one student, a fifth-grade girl, two days a week and to also work in the office of the Libyan Ministry of Justice four days a week. When she went to teach, she would pack her beloved desk-top computer in a bag on her back and much to the delight of her student, teach her how to use it. She couldn't depend on the salary from her jobs coming every month, but she continued with the hope that she would eventually be paid. While she was working for the government, Eman heard that some of her classmates from the Institute were getting scholarships from the *Green Book* Committee to study in the UK, another dream she had tucked away at the back of her mind.

"I had a relative who was in charge of choosing students, so my dad asked him about a scholarship. I received the application papers with the idea, if I was chosen, my brother would go with me since it was not proper for a woman to leave the country without a male relative for protection." When she told friends she was planning to go to England, they laughed. "Study abroad? We don't think so," they countered. Instead of disturbing Eman, their snide comments just added fuel to the fire of her determination. She completed a ream of paperwork for the scholarship, but when she was ready to turn it in, the Committee had changed. She was told to do it all over again. Not giving up, she did what was asked and re-submitted the forms.

While she was waiting to hear from the Committee, another road block was put in her way. One morning, after a year of employment at the Ministry, she was getting ready to leave for work when she heard that the Ministry building had been set on fire by anti-Qaddafi protesters. Her job no longer existed. She needed to find another place of employment. As she later said, "Lack of money controlled me a lot, and when I had some money, I couldn't keep it all for myself because I also wanted to help my dad and sisters." Coupled with the loss of income was the news that her application for a scholarship to Great Britain was refused. It was like herding sheep. When she had corralled one, another would slip away. Evidently, she did not have the necessary *wasta*, the important connections or favoritism, needed to receive a scholarship. In this case, it was lack of influence with someone on the *Green Book* Committee. The door to study in Great Britain had slammed shut, but Eman was determined to find another way to study abroad. But first she needed a decent job that would bring a regular salary. Even employment required wasta. Access to help-wanted ads and job search websites was as remote in Libya as travel to the planet of Mars. "I gave up on getting any favors and decided to move ahead by myself," she said. What happened next would forever change Eman's life.

We both looked up at the atomic clock on the wall of the conference room. It was about 3:30, time for her husband Sami to pick her up. Even though Libyan women were allowed to drive, Eman's family at home in Libya never had the money to provide an extra car, and now, too, Eman and Sami's finances were limited. She had to rely on her husband, with the kids in tow, or a lengthy ride on two buses. After a quick goodbye embrace, I sat down again in the student desk and listened to the last few minutes of the recording. That word *wasta* reminded me of how badly I wanted this privilege when we first arrived in Cairo to begin our four years at American University. A month in advance of our travel to Egypt, American University allowed us to ship a limited number of pounds of additional clothing, books, and toys for our family of five. We were desperate for the remnants of our American lives to arrive and comfort us, but they evidently were stuck at the sea port in Alexandria. "I want to play with my matchbox cars! I want my Barbie doll! I can't go to school without more clothes!" were pleas from our kids who were three, eight, and ten years old. We were told it wasn't possible to hurry up the process. Three months later, a university expediter, an Egyptian who had *wasta*, intervened. He went to Alexandria and gave the manager of shipment a bribe, *baksheesh*, of 50 Egyptian pounds. The *baksheesh* combined with the expediter's wasta worked. As I interacted with students from Arab Gulf countries after returning to the States, I saw examples of the power of their connections to the royal families in their countries. Many students had the promise of good jobs when they returned with degrees, no matter what US university or college they had graduated from. It was not like connections with important people didn't grease the wheels in the United States, but they were not as essential as *wasta* in the Middle East.

CHAPTER 3

Turning Point

"SISTERS AND BROTHERS ARE AS CLOSE AS HANDS AND FEET." THIS
ARABIC PROVERB APTLY DESCRIBES EMAN'S RELATIONSHIP TO HER OLDEST
BROTHER, MUNIR, AND MIDDLE BROTHER, RAMI. They both whole-
heartedly supported their sister's goals. Munir gave Eman rides
to work and paid for her computer classes. In the hunt for jobs,
Rami always stepped forward. After his sister had lost her job at
the Ministry, he discovered a job opening for a computer-savvy
person at a printing press where a friend of his was employed. He
encouraged her to apply. In spite of being a woman working only
with men, she was hired on the spot. Her intelligence and ability
to learn quickly impressed the owner and his three sons. Two of
the young men were friendly and talkative. The third son, Sami,
said "Good morning" and "How are you?" but nothing more. She
wondered about his quietness but assumed he was just shy. After
eight months of working hard and saving her salary, Eman resigned,
but her acquaintance with the owner's family would one day affect
her life again. Now she needed to devote her time to working
on admission to a university in Libya. If she could complete her
bachelor's degree, she would be promised a university lectureship
in addition to the opportunity to study abroad.

A relative told her about Azzaytoonah University, 55 kilometers away. She could complete her full undergraduate degree by taking fourteen classes during two years of study and preparing a graduate project to fulfill requirements for a four-year university degree. Azzaytoonah, supported by Qaddafi, was founded for African students from countries like Eritrea, Ethiopia, and Congo. These foreign students had free tuition plus a stipend and were joined by Libyan students who had to be *Green Book* Committee members. If she possessed that coveted card of membership, Azzaytoonah would be a wonderful opportunity even though she would have to spend a twelve-hour day commuting and studying.

Again, *wasta* was the abracadabra that could open the door to the coveted card. It's not common for a woman to step outside her docile role to ask for a man's help, but with head held high and her usual determination, Eman contacted a co-worker at the Ministry. He was unable to help, but he referred her to someone else who provided the necessary application for membership in the Green Book Committee. She submitted the paperwork, and much to her surprise, she was accepted and received official approval. As soon as she obtained the card, she was faced with the next problem: How would she get to the university? None of the schedules of her brothers and sisters with cars fit the times she needed to travel, she had no money to buy her own car, and there was no public transportation from her home. She finally found a bus going from Tarhuna to the campus, but it was designated only for university employees. Although she was just a lowly student, she decided to ask the bus driver for permission.

"I found two bus drivers, one who would pick me up on the roadside between 4 and 5 a.m. and deliver me to the next bus stop which was on the main road. From there, the second bus driver allowed me to board a bus for university employees. My classes were at different times of day, but I would need to stay the entire day. My mom woke me up early each day, and my dad drove me to the bus stop in the dark and waited with me until the bus came."

The first day of her journey began on a cold, dark morning in September. The bus came at 4:45 a.m. All went well until she boarded the second bus. All but two of the riders were men. All eyes were on her. She sat down in an empty seat next to a window. "I remember looking outside and asking myself the same questions the passengers and many of my relatives were asking: 'Where am I going? What am I doing on this bus? Is this the proper thing to do?'" Her answer, a mantra that was always in the back of her mind, came to the surface: "I'm using this bus as a ladder to climb up to my goals. I believe in myself and in God. I am confident."

After a few kilometers, the men on the bus resumed their routine of singing ribald songs and telling jokes. Eman ignored them and fixed her eyes on the rows of pine and olive trees along the road. When they arrived at Azzaytoona University, she joined the line of workers and got off the bus to walk to the entrance. Just as she entered the double doors, a middle-aged woman blocked the way, stuck out her tongue, and shook her finger in Eman's face.

"I saw you coming on the employee bus. What are you doing here? You can't come on this bus!"

Eman was shocked. She took a step back and a moment to absorb the affront.

Then looking the woman directly in the eyes, she said, "It's not your bus. I'm not taking anything away from you. *Ma'shallah*! I've never met a person like you." Eman turned and walked away to find her first class. The two women avoided each other after that.

The travel and studies from Sunday through Thursday became routine. As is usual in Muslim countries, weekends included the holy day of Friday plus Saturday. One Saturday about half-way through the first semester, Eman's uncle had a very important telephone call from a friend of his, the owner of the printing press where Eman had worked. After exchanging greetings and small talk, his friend had a special request.

"My son Sami is interested in marrying your niece, Eman. Would you ask her to consider him as her future husband?" The request was promptly relayed to Eman. What a surprise! Sami, who was thirty years old, was the shy one of the three sons who worked in the family printing business. She didn't really know him at all, and marriage was the last thing on her bucket list. During the past few years, other suitors had approached her family to ask about marriage. "I was always thinking about jobs, traveling abroad, and trying to find a way to get there, so I said 'No' to their proposals. On the other hand, I had sisters and cousins who were getting married. I was twenty-three, and women in my country usually marry between twenty and thirty. Maybe it was my time." She told her uncle she would need some time to consider the proposal and let him know soon.

Weighing both sides was part of her thought process. "If I said 'Yes', how would it affect my life and my dreams? I really had no idea. Would I be the same person? Would I have to change? Would my husband want to take the journey overseas with me? This was a big risk. I prayed that God would guide me to do what was best." She recited a special prayer, *Salat-I-Istikhara*, to ask Allah for help in making her decision, the same prayer used by Nisren in other situations: "Oh, Allah! If in your knowledge, this marriage is good for my religion, my livelihood, and my affairs, immediate and in the future, then ordain it for me, make it easy for me, and bless it for me. . . .And ordain for me the good wherever it may be and make me content with it."

I was skeptical when Eman described her decision-making process. Accepting God's will for her life might very well run counter to her determination to succeed in her own goals, I thought. On the other hand, I knew it was central to her belief in Islam, a word literally meaning "submission to the will of Allah." The Koran asserts that the only correct human response to God is total submission which, in turn, brings peace and harmony. Matters of personal will, choice, and freedom blur against the will of Allah. Seeking God's direction isn't just an Islamic belief; it is a common precept in both Christianity and Judaism. The challenge is its effect on one's actions. It had always bothered me when the phrase "It was God's will" was used to explain away disasters like hurricanes and floods. To me, this attitude paralyzed efforts to look at root causes and make changes. Asking for God's help in discerning what actions to take was a more acceptable interpretation of "God's will." According to some Christian theologians, Allah demands submission, and God seeks cooperation.

My own experience in the Middle East opened my eyes to the tragic results of blind obedience to the concept of *en sha'allah*, "God willing." In Cairo, our family lived in an American university villa complete with a gardener, Ayoub, a kind, hard-working man who was part of our daily lives. Ayoub was being treated for bilharzia, a parasitic infection contracted from working barefoot in soil irrigated with Nile River water. One day when I apologized to him for our four-year-old's destruction of flower pots with his tricycle, Ayoub responded with a smile and "*ma'alesh*," never mind. Then he told me his wife had just given birth to a little girl, but the baby was sick. When I found that no doctor had seen the newborn, I suggested he take the baby to the university's free clinic where he was also being treated. His response was "*en sha'allah*," God willing. Two weeks later, he told me the baby had died. My unspoken reaction was "Why didn't you take her to see the doctor? She might have lived." As I learned more about the acceptance of God's will in Egyptian life, I also realized that it comforted people facing illness, death, and poverty in a developing country. These trials were considered part of God's purpose in one's life and surrender to His will would lead to paradise after death.

So what would be the result of Eman's special prayers? I pondered the fine line between blind acceptance of God's will and the discernment of what God wants for one's future. I could see that her decision to marry at this time could endanger her path to study abroad when she had worked so hard for her dream. It all depended, in my mind, on her prospective groom's openness to her goals.

"What if this new husband of yours didn't want you to study outside Libya? You couldn't go unless he accompanied you, could you?" She laughed away my serious questions.

"If I married Sami and he wanted me to stay in Libya, that would have to be OK. I might not accept it at first, but with time I would. I believe that Allah had led me to the best choice," she replied.

I dug into my limited mental trove of Arabic and found my favorite expression of disbelief: "*Ya salaam*! Wow! That's hard for me to understand, Eman."

She was amused at my concern but reiterated her willingness to throw away all of her persistence and hard work for marriage to someone who might not agree to support her goal of study in the US. This was not a seventeen-year-old Nisren in Iraq, who shyly agreed to marry the handsome suitor who would get to know her, so she would fall in love with him by the time of the marriage. When she got married, Eman was a strong twenty-five-year-old woman who had never lost her focus on the future. I now realized the strength of her obedience to Islam. As she said in childhood, "To be a good girl, I had to be a good Muslim." If I could revise her life story, I would have her interview Sami, just as a prospective employer would, to ask him if he would approve her goal of studying in the United States. But evidently, this was not proper. She had to make her decision without the facts.

Added to her prayers was a rational consideration of both sides of her decision. Marriage was a turning point for all Libyan women, basically the end of their freedom to socialize with friends of their choice and the beginning of heavy family obligations. The amount of socializing also depended on your tribe. Sami's tribal group was very social. Every occasion that marked a holiday, a birth, a wedding, an illness, or a death required preparation of food, purchase of gifts, invitations to all relatives from both sides of the family, and approval of your husband if it involved a friend and not a relative. Because these were large events, there were no opportunities to have private conversations with just friends.

Pushing aside her doubts and unanswered questions, she was feeling positive about marriage. "There's a *hadith*, or saying, of Muhammad in the Koran that guides parents," she said. "When someone comes to marry your daughter, if you are satisfied that he is of good character and religious, then you should say 'Yes.'" She knew that Sami was a good person from a good family. He had accomplished a Koranic study degree and had been teaching the holy book for almost seven years. Working at the printing press was not his only job. He also did the physical labor required to maintain the family's farm outside the city. He spent many hours planting and harvesting wheat and other crops. He was also a handsome young man of medium height with a kind face, dark brown eyes, and a high forehead.

After talking to her family for several days about his proposal, Eman agreed to the engagement with the caveat that the five days of engagement celebration would not happen until Sami finished building their home, which would take almost two years, and would give her time to graduate from the university. Libyan men marry a few years older than women because they must save money to buy or build a house and pay for the bracelets, rings, and other gold gifts to the bride. As soon as Eman agreed, a contract was drawn up by an imam, a religious leader from the mosque, who came to Sami's house. The bride and groom were not present but were represented by male family members. Two items were agreed upon: the amount of money due to the bride before marriage, the *mukadem*, and the sum of money given to the bride if there was a divorce, the *moahker*. These sums are token considerations to fulfill religious requirements and validate the marriage. Once the guardians of the bride and groom shook hands, the imam led the men in reciting the opening chapter of the Koran. The couple was now legally and religiously married. The only time Eman saw Sami before the wedding night was after the legal ceremony where they met and talked briefly. Contact with her new family came from occasional visits from Sami's mother and his niece. The whirlwind of celebration and the actual wedding night came later. Two of Sami's brothers would celebrate their marriages at the same time as he and Eman, so the expense of all the big events would not be so great.

Getting married in Libya, as in Iraq, involved clearly defined roles, but the number of Libyan customs would rival the length of Qaddafi's *Green Book*. Just as in Nisren's situation as a Shiite Kurd in Iraq, a Sunni woman in Libya must be a virgin. Eman told me that men, too, are discouraged from having sex before marriage but added a rather impossible qualification: "Men should learn to be patient and not to think about women until they are ready to get married. This way, Allah will bless a couple's lives because they have chosen the right path, which is marriage." She told me some men may sneak off to Tunisia to visit a prostitute, but there is no loosening of rules for women. In fact, it is dangerous for a woman to even be seen with a man before marriage because there will be suspicion that she is not pure. In the past, some women who were suspected of not being virgins were killed by family members to preserve the honor of the family. A bride-to-be may not even have seen her future husband because Sunni Islam restricts contact between men and women before the wedding night. After the formal engagement, conversations by telephone are allowed but no visual or physical contact. Eman did not have the good fortune to be wooed by her fiancé as Nisren had in the many private conversations that her father allowed with Raad when they were engaged.

"What about love?" I asked.

"It comes when the couple gets to know each other after marriage," she said.

With the decision to marry Sami checked off Eman's to-do list, other items took precedence. Arduous days of study and commuting filled her life, but she also yearned for a better acquaintance with Sami through telephone conversations. Although she visited with Sami's mother and his niece, she did not see her future husband until the wedding night. Just a few bread crumbs of knowledge were sprinkled by Sami's once-a-month phone calls, which lasted for less than five minutes. "He was just not used to talking to a woman," she explained. She pushed this disappointment to the back of her mind to concentrate on her university studies. The only pothole in the road to graduation was the professor who was appointed as the advisor on her required senior thesis. He would not accept the time constraints that her daily travel presented. He demanded that their required meetings be at a time he set, usually after the bus came to take her home.

"You are always bringing me excuses," he scolded. "I regret ever having agreed to advise you."

Her response was rapid-fire. "You don't have to be my advisor. I can find another one. I can't stay late, or I'll miss my bus."

Surprised at the quick retort from a woman, he backed down, continued to oversee her work, and finally approved her for graduation. Completing Institute requirements coupled with preparation for the wedding necessitated exciting but serious multitasking; however,

Eman wasn't going to forego a graduation celebration after all her hard work. She planned a small party at the Institute with some special guests: the two bus drivers who provided her much-needed transportation.

The week before the actual wedding was a panorama of well-planned events. It starred Eman in a once-in-a-lifetime experience scripted like a movie: an introduction of the major players, rising action leading to the climax, falling action, and a denouement that resolved all issues. In this case, the cast was comprised of hundreds of relatives and friends. Eman's family was expected to prepare the food for invited guests from both families during the five days of parties and feasting. Several weeks prior to the official Monday that began the festivities, Sami sent her more than $2,000 to buy new clothes, from underwear to dresses and shoes plus cosmetics, perfumes, shampoos, and lotions. Newly-married brides must dress up for a year after the wedding, so what Westerners might call "cocktail dresses" were among the purchases. Eman added money she had been saving to the groom's gift to be able to start her married life with nothing borrowed, nothing blue, but everything new.

"It took me several weeks to shop, but I enjoyed it," she said. All of the new items were put in decorated baskets that were delivered to the groom's house before Invitation Day, the kick-off of the week's events. Some of her friends were invited with written invitations and others by word of mouth at a party of close friends and neighbors at her house. Women and men were separated at all of the occasions. Laughing, sexual advice, and story-telling tickled the tension that built up to Thursday, the wedding night, termed in direct language as "the opening night." Not only must the bride be beautifully coiffed and made-up, but her body must be just as beautiful, so Eman had one personal chore to accomplish on Monday, and a somewhat painful one: waxing to remove hair on face, arms, legs, and private parts of her body. "You must be shiny," she joked.

A long line of cars with horns blasting pulled up in front of Eman's home on Tuesday evening. Each car, driven by a male relative, carried female guests from Sami's family, dressed in glamorous Western gowns but covered head-to-toe by their long, black abayas. Eman's father and brothers received the group. When the women got out of the cars, the men lifted decorated baskets on to their heads. All the items Eman had purchased were displayed in the baskets, including the gold bracelets, rings, and necklaces Sami had bought as gifts to the bride. The women swayed to a rhythmic drum beat as they entered the party room to place their baskets on display tables. The guests also were on display when they removed their abayas to reveal their dresses, some long and some short, and their intricate gold jewelry. Eman, dressed in the required traditional pink was seated on a platform for everyone to admire. The voluminous gown was folded up into cushion-like forms at the back and hips and decorated with embroidery and jewels. When everyone has assembled, one of Sami's female relatives took the basket of gold and put the necklaces, bracelets, and rings on the bride. Guests were served treats in a specific order beginning with water when they arrived and then almond juice with coconut, wedding cookies, and tea with more sweets. After everyone from the two families had introduced themselves, the drumming and dancing began. Two women drummers beat their fingers and palms on goblet-shaped drums, rising and falling in rhythm while other women sang songs that had been sung at weddings for hundreds of years. Other women clapped, and some circled their hips and twirled their hands in harmony to the drum beats. The more excited the crowd grew, the louder the drums beat. Eman, in the dress that weighed ten pounds, remained seated but joined the clapping and singing.

Wednesday was henna day, a time to celebrate joy and good luck and a night to again don the heavy pink dress. In the afternoon, Eman's hands and feet were decorated with the unique design reserved for brides. After her first anniversary, she would be permitted to change her henna pattern slightly, using creative designs to decorate around her heel or knuckle. She sat patiently in a chair while her cousin, a henna expert, ground the leaves and prepared the dark red paste that would be applied over the elaborate stenciled pattern. Gathered around her were female friends and family members and the requisite amount of food to make it a special event. It was a time to be thoughtful. Sami had told her he would call today, so she considered what she wanted to say to him. Would she tell him now about her planned study in another country?

Her grandmother, Amna, was seated nearby where she could clearly see her favorite granddaughter. As Eman sat very still with outstretched arms, she looked at the old woman. Tears were flowing down the wrinkles in her cheeks as she thought about not having Eman close to her at night to comfort her in case she woke up and to bring her hot water in the morning before prayer time. The weight of all she would miss dawned on Eman, too, as she shed tears with her grandmother.

In thinking about this poignant moment in a later interview, she said, "Sometimes people who love you give you a tough love. My grandmother, may Allah have mercy on her soul, was one of those people. When I was little I didn't realize how much she loved me, but I found out she was hard on me because she cared about me. I think she hid her tender feelings because she needed to prove she was more than equal to a man in spite of the tough environment and her husband's death"

When evening came and the henna was dry, it was party time. More than one hundred female guests packed into the courtyard of the house, and the same number of men arrived at a tent specially set up outside. Torches lit up the night as the men sang, danced, and drummed. A cacophony of sound rang out until almost 2:30 in the morning as the women's voices competed with the men's. Guests were given small gifts of sweets to take home with them. Although she was exhausted from all the festivities, she found it difficult to sleep because Sami had not called. She was nervous about her wedding night. Was Sami nervous too? she wondered.

The height of wedding festivities had finally arrived. Thursday marked the wedding night and preparations for it. Eight other brides were at the beauty salon when Eman arrived early in the morning. It was necessary to make reservations two months in advance, so enough make-up artists and hair stylists would be ready to transform each woman for the most important day in her life. The male relatives weren't left out; they were served a large meal in the afternoon at a groom's party. About 6 p.m., after hair coloring, styling, facial, and bold make-up, Eman returned home to put on her Western-style white wedding dress, all her gold jewelry, and a small tiara on her head. In order to receive women guests, she sat in a decorated chair, so all could see her transformation. After admiration at her beauty and, of course, more food, singing, and dancing, Eman's brother arrived to take her to her new home where Sami was waiting. This ritual denoted the official departure from her parents' home to join the groom and his tribe.

A white tent-like robe was placed over Eman, so no one could see her as the car drove slowly to their new house where her husband was waiting. In our interview, her desire to be private left the rest to my imagination. In my mind, I see her being led into the bedroom to sit on a chair and wait for Sami. Her hands are folded together in her lap trying to compose herself. The white covering is hot as she takes short breaths. Questions are colliding in her mind: What will it be like to have a man touch me? Will "the opening" be painful? What will

I say? Will my quiet husband say anything? Will we talk about the future? Can I finally tell him about my ambition to study abroad?

My imagination takes hold again. I see Sami entering the bedroom, walking to the bed where Eman is seated, and removing the white cover to reveal his bride. He draws a deep breath, holds it for a moment, and whispers, "You're beautiful." He continues to grasp the white cloth in his hands, and instead of looking straight at Eman, his eyes are shyly trained on a bouquet of flowers on the table next to the bed. She takes the cloth from his hands and folds it. Then she looks directly at his face for the first time. His dark brown eyes, straight nose, and strong chin prove that he is as handsome as she had thought His eyes meet hers for a few seconds. He reaches out a hand that is quickly met by hers. The long-awaited wedding night has begun. It is a private time for both of them: a time for awkward intimacy and the newness of just getting to know each other.

CHAPTER 4

Afterwards

SLEEP WAS REPLACED BY AN EARLY MORNING CONVERSATION THAT RELIEVED EMAN'S NEED FOR THE ANSWER TO HER MOST IMPORTANT QUESTION. She understood now that Sami had not called her because he just didn't know what to say. His shyness was endearing to her and prepared her to pose the question that would determine her future and Sami's.

"What would you think about going abroad with me to study?"

She waited for an answer, but no words were spoken. He didn't look shocked. Instead, he was smiling and nodding his head affirmatively. Evidently he had already heard about her goal from his friends. What a relief! Her prayers had worked in her favor.

A few hours later, a knock at the door alerted the sleepless couple that another day of obligations was ahead of them. Her mother-in-law and sister-in-law were there to help her get dressed for a large breakfast with special wedding pastries, followed by visits from guests who could not attend the wedding party and dinner with her new family. This would require full make-up and changing dresses to greet the guests and serve them food. In the meantime, Sami went to the mosque to offer prayers of gratitude to Allah. When this day was finished, the official wedding was at an end.

A honeymoon? Not for Eman and Sami because other tasks faced them in the next few weeks. Greeting and preparing for guests barely gave them little time for intimacy. When they had been married for one week, they followed the custom of buying a live sheep to give as a gift to his family in addition to giving sweets and other gifts to a small number of close relatives and friends. Wearing traditional clothes, they visited a different house each might to introduce themselves as a newly married couple. With that week behind them, they were confronted by Ramadan, the month of fasting from eating, drinking, and having sexual relations from dawn to sundown. Added to her schedule was cooking special food for *iftar*, the breaking of the fast at sunset, and making time for neighbors to visit and talk to her and the other newlyweds in Sami's family.

Since Eman was now a member of his family, she had to develop a good relationship with her mother-in-law, Mariam, a diabetic who was ready to relax from doing all the cooking for her family and her husband's construction crew of Egyptians. "I have three new daughters-in-law," she said, "so they can make dinner for the whole family and clean up afterwards." Starting in the second month of their marriage, Eman was scheduled with one of the other brides to meet at her mother-in-law's house at noon to cook, stay until 3 or 4 p.m., take a nap at home, and return to the house to serve the meal and clean up. "I was shocked at the schedule but couldn't say no." She managed to fit her own household chores and her teaching hours into the busy day. A negative response to the wishes of her mother-in-law would have resulted in being cast out of the family and unsupported by it. She acknowledged the ever-present need to accept whatever you are dealt: "You can't change some things at the end of the day just because you don't like them." She knew that phase of her married life would be over at some point, and in this case, it lasted one year.

The passing of that first year marked a significant event that changed the family's lives. It was a tradition for Sami's family to go to Mecca, Saudi Arabia, on a yearly pilgrimage to visit the holy Islamic sites. *Umra*, sometimes called "the little pilgrimage," is recommended for all Muslims but not required as is the *Haj* or "big pilgrimage," which is a once-in-a-lifetime obligation for those who are physically and financially able to perform it. Eman was excited about joining the family for this spiritual experience. She and Sami had thought of having a baby during their first year of marriage but decided to postpone pregnancy until after the three-week trip. Some of the teaching money she had been saving for household furnishings became money for the pilgrimage. She had to buy some personal items and simple white dresses and headscarves to signify the shedding of all signs of wealth and societal connections. Whatever she bought for herself, she also bought for Mariam.

Just two months before their departure for Saudi Arabia, Mariam fell and broke her leg. Because they did not trust Libyan surgeons, she was taken to Tunisia where an orthopedic surgeon repaired the leg but required that she use a wheelchair to return to Libya. The family worried that she would not be able to meet the physical demands required of each pilgrim: a visit to the *Ka'bah*, the holy stone that marks the place that Muhammed received the Koran, and completion of seven circuits between two small mountains. Could they manage the wheelchair and take good care of her during the many steps involved in the pilgrimage? After several months of recuperation and removal of the cast from her leg, Mariam convinced the family that she was strong enough to make the trip. It might be the last time she would be able to do it, she insisted. They finally agreed, made the necessary preparations, and embarked on the four-hour flight to Mecca.

Tragedy struck on the third day of their pilgrimage. The women in the family, who stayed in separate hotel rooms from the men, felt a spiritual bond as they prayed together each day and chatted about their experiences at night. In spite of her infirmities, Mariam seemed absorbed in her inner, spiritual life. In one of their late-night conversations, she asked the group, "Do you know of women who died here in Medina during *Umra*? How wonderful to be buried here as part of a final journey!" Her family dismissed her comments as wishful thinking. Like all Muslims, she believed that her present life was only a trial preparation for afterlife with a day of judgment, a choice of heaven or hell, and the possibility of resurrection.

On the third morning in Medina, her mother-in-law suggested they say their morning prayers out-of-doors instead of going inside the mosque. They helped her to get out of the wheelchair. She knelt on a prayer rug with Eman on her left and Eman's sister-in-law on her right. After the prayers, when the women stood up to help her back into the wheelchair, they found her slumped over on the rug.

Eman wanted to get her some water, but her sister-in-law told her to quickly find her father-in-law inside the mosque where the men were praying.

"I found him, held his hand, and took him to her, but she was already dead." Her father-in-law lifted her body into the wheelchair and called an ambulance. Sami's mother would have the wish she had mentioned the night before. She would be interred in Al-Baqi Cemetery, located southeast of the Prophet's Mosque where many of the Prophet Muhammad's companions and relatives were buried. Her wish had come true.

In Islam, it is preferable to inter the body on the same day that the death occurs, but in this situation there wasn't time, so the family made plans for the next day. Eman helped the women wash the body for burial and wrap it in a clean white cloth. "I had never seen a dead person before," she said. "Her face was purple. I touched her body and touched the hair she had combed just a few hours ago."

After preparing the body, Eman's involvement in her mother-in-law's death was complete. Women are not allowed to accompany men on the journey to Medina. In the meantime, the family at home in Libya were not told of Mariam's death. It was a tradition to shield relatives and friends from the direct truth about death or any catastrophe. "They wouldn't believe us because of the shock, so we told family she had a stroke and was hospitalized. People called to say prayers for her and ask about her. Our answer was 'She's in intensive care.'" When they returned to Libya, the truth was told to relatives and friends, who accepted the news with mourning cries and screams.

Life settled down into a more normal routine when Eman and Sami returned to their new home in Tarhuna. Sami went back to his job at the press, and although they were still considered newly-weds, the social obligations lessened. They made good on their plan to become pregnant, so Eman began saving her teaching money for the birth of their baby. Having a child did not deter her from reaching the goal of study abroad. The everyday quality of married life and work did not last long, however, because the fabric of Qaddafi's Libya was starting to rip apart.

CHAPTER 5

What Is the Truth?

THE SMELL OF LAMB, MINT, DILL, AND PARSLEY STILL LINGERED IN THE KITCHEN OF THEIR NEW HOUSE IN AL KHADRA VILLAGE. It was almost 8 p.m. on February 22, 2011. Twenty-eight-year old Eman and her husband's niece Susu had finished washing the dishes after cooking a hasty meal of soup. Susu had done most of the preparation because the odor of cooking food still nauseated Eman, who was four months pregnant. Meal preparation had become a hasty task because electricity was sporadic and cooking gas was in short supply since the first major protests and violence had begun in Benghazi a week before. Inspired by Arab Spring revolts in neighboring Tunisia and Egypt, hundreds of Libyans had gathered outside a Benghazi police station waving signs and shouting "Down with Qaddafi!" and "Release the prisoners!" The revolt quickly spread to Tripoli, just 60 miles west of Tarhuna.

Sami was sitting on a cushion in the living room of their new house, fingering his prayer beads as he stared at the flickering light on a large TV screen accompanied by the half-tones of Arabic music. He had heard that Supreme Leader Qaddafi was going to give an important TV speech to the Libyan nation that night.

"Maybe we'll learn what's really happening," he thought to himself. Like a fulfilled promise, the TV screen was suddenly focused on the green Libyan flag and the music changed to the marching sounds of the national anthem. Eman and Susu hurried into the living room and settled onto cushions next to Sami. Eman placed her hands on her belly to comfort and protect the baby boy inside her.

Suddenly, Qaddafi's Botox-puffed face under a shock of curly, dyed black hair jumped onto the screen with a blast of words and full volume.

"Who are you? Who are you?" he shouted. "You are the drug-takers, *jihadis*, and rats," he ranted, threatening the demonstrators in the streets. In the background, a crowd of supporters jumped up and down waving green flags in response to his invective.

"You people taking *helluwassa* drugs have been made crazy!"

Slamming his fist on the podium, he shouted, "*Zenga! Zenga!* We will cleanse Libya inch by inch, alleyway by alleyway, person by person, street by street, house by house!"

Eman shivered and pulled her shawl closer around her shoulders and over her belly. Sami leaned forward, his nose almost touching the TV screen, as if his eyes could pierce through Qaddafi and learn the truth of what was taking place in his country.

"Not knowing what to believe was the worst thing," Eman said. "The military leaders were telling made-up stories about who we were fighting. Qaddafi wanted us to believe it was people on drugs who were raping and looting. When he said, 'Let's go to this city or that place where the opposition is taking young girls,' it was a way of recruiting more fighters."

Fear of what could happen if they did not fight the rebels was continually stirred up in other TV speeches. Qaddafi's son warned, "If the revolution starts, forget about cooking gas, electricity, and you will see what the country will look like." This was followed by Qaddafi, seemingly at his wit's end, shouting, "I will make this whole country burn like hell."

The truth had been always hard to come by during the four decades the tyrant was in power. No one could talk badly in public about the Supreme Leader because spies were everywhere and could quickly put a citizen in prison or hang him in public. The same "eyes on us" that Nisren experienced as a Kurd in Iraq restrained the Libyan populace.

When I asked Eman if she had grown up with fear of Qaddafi's regime, she seemed surprised. "I didn't even realize I had fear. I lived in a big family outside the city without even knowing what was happening politically. My dad worked building houses, not working in the government, but my uncle who worked with the army always had new cars and money. I remember admiring all the things he had. But no, I wasn't afraid because my vision was limited to my own dream of an education."

As I listened to Eman talk about the routine of her everyday life as a child, I realized that the business of living goes on in spite of the threat of chaos and revolution. Libyans went to work or school, ate their lunches, and went home to their families. There were universities and businesses. Most people worried about making sure their kids got a good education and lived better lives than their parents. Jobs were available, but who you knew was important to finding the best job. Government bureaucracy got in the way, but there were ways to get around it. When you didn't know anything different, life was tolerable and could even be considered good.

As she looked back on those days, she realized what was hidden beneath the daily routine. People were silent about the Qaddafi regime's bloody secrets until the revolution finally exploded. Then everyone was telling the hidden stories of mass murder, sexual exploitation, and corruption. But were these stories true? It was difficult to sort out the facts from what some believed were fiction. Many Libyans still worshipped the hero whose image stared down at them from every public building and came alive in strategically-placed statues. They had memorized his *Green Book* as children and shouted for him in the public square when he gave a speech. After all, he had built public works projects, including the Great Man-Made River, a network of underground pipelines bringing water from ancient underground aquifers in the Sahara to the coast of Libya, and built schools, hospitals, and universities. Education and medical treatment were free. Having a home was considered a human right. People had enough food. Others considered Qaddafi, who once had himself crowned the "King of Kings" of Africa, a madman who had slaughtered over 1,000 prisoners at Abu Salim prison and a lecher whose sexual escapades had destroyed the lives of hundreds of young women.

A citizen's allegiance to Qaddafi depended on where one lived and the history of that area. For centuries, Libya's three regions— Cyrenaica to the east, Tripolitania to the west on the Mediterranean coast, and Fezzan to the south in the desert—were separate territories with unique experiences of Qaddafi's leadership. People in the east had never accepted Qaddafi, who punished them by neglecting their capital city Benghazi, so it was natural for the rebellion to begin there. Eastern Libyans remembered the time Benghazi was the center of power before Qaddafi's Al-Fattah Revolution led to what they thought was a downward spiral into ruin. People from Cyrenaica and Tripolitania were mostly Arabs descended from Muslims in the seventh century. People from Fezzan were more African than Arab, with ancestral roots from the nomadic Tuareg, who spread across the unmarked borders of the Sahara into Algeria and Niger. Hundreds of years of trade among the three regions had mixed up the regional identity, but their roots remained.

Tarhuna, Eman's birthplace, was a city boasting a good relationship with Qaddafi, but Sami's family, with its printing business in Tripoli, had always been silently against him. These opposite viewpoints caused her and Sami to seek even harder for the truth of what was happening in a country that, in their minds, had always been peaceful and secure.

Not knowing the facts about events led to visible divisions between those who supported Qaddafi and those who supported the revolution and were against him. People who favored him started flying the solid green flag while others restored the striped flag that represented Libya before Qaddafi. Eman's city of Tarhuna immediately raised the green flag to represent their approval of Qaddafi. Each city flew the flag of its loyalty.

"Family members had big fights because some were against and some were for Qaddafi," Eman explained. "Any conversation about politics turned people against each other. At weddings or funerals, people actually had arguments and fights because some came wearing green if they supported Qaddafi and others wore stripes if they supported the revolution against him."

Apparently, access to guns was the seed of the killings that were taking place. Each major city had an armory that could be accessed by the military. People who were pro-Qaddafi were given access to the gun storage and then weapons were distributed to those whose duty it was to kill the "drug-takers," who were the revolutionaries in actuality. In the days before the revolution, guns were licensed and strictly controlled. They were mostly held by those in the military. Suddenly, everyone had a gun in his house. Requests to return guns to the cities' armories were to no avail. Instead people stocked more guns in their houses. Many people who grabbed guns had never used one before. With the gun came a need to dress in something that looked military. Next was the need to organize movement throughout the country. All at once, there were hastily set-up security gates on all the highways, most of which were only two lanes.

"If you had a gun and some kind of uniform, you had a job," Eman said. "You could be pro- or anti-Qaddafi. These people would shout 'Stop! What's your name? We need to search your car.' It was scary."

Qaddafi used money to turn people to his side. Government workers had their salaries raised, and people without jobs were given employment and salaries. Teenagers who had just completed high school were recruited by military leaders, who picked them up in buses. They were told that they would be paid money up front and more money when they fought the drug-takers. "There were teenagers with guns bigger than they were," Eman explained. "Social media wasn't common, but the TV videos drove us crazy. They showed people in court, judges in blue robes, and prisoners with death sentences dressed in orange pants and shirts. In one video, a man who was charged with taking drugs confesses and says that a leader made them go house to house to cut off women's breasts and then have a party to celebrate," Eman continued. "The videos made you feel like these people needed to be judged and killed." In spite of the fear and horror that was being instilled in the minds of Libyans, the question of truth was always present. Who was right, and who was wrong?

From the day the revolution began, February 15, 2011, there were shortages of cooking gas and petrol for cars. Unruly lines of people queued up without respect for who was first. "We had to save 20 liters of gasoline, so Sami could take me to a private hospital to have the baby," Eman said. "I had saved my teaching salary because I didn't want to have the necessary C-section in a public hospital that was filled with the injured. I wanted a private hospital close to Tripoli, so we would be safe."

Five months later on the sixth day of fasting for Ramadan, baby Saif was born in a private clinic with its own generator and air conditioning. The bombing in nearby Tripoli was still audible above the comforting noise of the small air conditioner in her hospital room where she stayed for three nights. Always aware of the rules of Islam, she knew that it was permissible to eat and drink during this time and later make up the required fasting for Ramadan. Her sister-in-law provided her with food and helped care for Saif because nurses were not allowed to care for the babies. When Eman came home, she was confronted with the lack of electricity and bottled gas. Meals had to be cooked over wood fires, just as her grandmother might have done many years ago. "I just wished I could take Saif away to another planet," she said, "but this was my life, no options, no other choices."

Unfortunately, she was on the losing side in the battles she was fighting. An infection and fever prevented her from breastfeeding, the pain from surgery disabled her, and she struggled unsuccessfully against the strength of social obligations. It was a tradition to receive and feed guests at a birth celebration during the first week at home. A separate bedroom large enough to seat and feed more than twenty people was prepared. Her extended family assisted with preparation of food from the limited supply that was available. Eman, trying hard to be sociable in spite of her condition, was propped up in bed with Saif in her arms. One of the elderly guests complained that she had no cold water to drink: "You have that big freezer and no cold water? How come?" Eman remembered thinking but not saying, "This is *my* life, isn't it? I just had a C-section and can't walk, and you're asking me to find you cold water?"

Social obligations and tradition continued to take precedence over the dangers of the revolution that was enveloping the country. The new mother was expected to organize and produce a baby shower for more than fifty guests from both families several weeks after delivering the baby. Although Eman was still weak, she started preparing the necessary food for the event, using money she had saved for lamb and cooking gas. While she was rinsing the meat, she received a call from her sister with bad news. One of her nephews had been in a bad accident and had to be taken to Tunisia for treatment. That was the end of the baby shower. "I decided we just needed to pray for him to live. I was not going through with the baby shower." The nephew was in a coma for twenty-one days, recovered, and was brought to Eman's family home to continue recuperating. Another obligation fulfilled.

The joy of bringing baby Saif into the world was tempered by the chaos all around her: "Beautiful buildings destroyed; no electricity, petrol, or cooking gas; and people who used to get along with each other now fighting one another." She came to the point of believing that peace was more important than who was leading the country. "I found myself wishing we could have just one day with Qaddafi as leader, so we could again experience security and safety. When people asked me are you for or against Qaddafi, I would say I'm in the middle. I don't like to talk politics. I just want the country returned to what it was before."

Freedom was a word that stirred the hearts of the rebels, but it was also a difficult concept to understand when people had never experienced it. There had been no freedom of the press, freedom to assemble, freedom to elect officials, freedom to express dissent, or freedom to know the truth of what was happening. They had lived for four decades in a dictatorship that ignored leadership by anyone but Qaddafi. There were no institutions and no political infrastructure. "Some people thought that freedom meant you could come to work at any time and do anything you wanted to do. They forgot the need to work hard to establish some organization in the country," Eman said. "Many of the people who were against Qaddafi had lived or studied outside the country, so they had seen what life could be like in a free country. I had no idea of the true meaning of freedom, and at that point I didn't know if I ever would," she added.

CHAPTER 6

The Great Adventure

CHILDBIRTH IN THE MIDST OF LACK OF WATER, FRESH FOOD, PETROL, AND COOKING OIL DIDN'T DETER EMAN FROM WORKING ON HER GOAL OF STUDY ABROAD. When her scholarship was first approved months before the revolution, she was given the choice of studying in England, Australia, New Zealand, Switzerland, Canada, or the United States.

"My friends still didn't believe I would really go abroad. They didn't understand how I could move so far away from family and friends," she said. Again, decisions were made only after praying for guidance from Allah plus gathering information on the internet for the facts about studying in each country. Her search was limited to the few hours the internet café was open. Her first choice, Great Britain, was closer to home, but she found it had stiff requirements for language proficiency, so she decided the United States was the best choice although it seemed very far away. A friend of her husband's suggested Denver, Colorado, where they could get an I-20, the document necessary for a student visa, from a specific language school that he had attended. She would travel on an F-1 visa and Sami and Saif on F-2 visas. This type of visa would allow Sami to study English but would prohibit him working in the US. In order to receive the visa, Eman had to show evidence of financial resources sufficient to support Sami and their son. As a rule, a prospective student must document a bank account with about $5,000 for a spouse and $3,500 for each child. In this case, however, the Libyan scholarship would provide the necessary financial support and the documents. The agency that handles the actual disbursement of money, the Canadian Bureau of International Education (CBIE), estimated that in 2011, two thousand Libyan students were studying in English-language and university program in the US. Colorado was home to nearly 400 of them, the most of any state.

It was difficult to make contact with the school on the internet, and Eman had no credit card that would allow her to pay the necessary application fee. An education service in Libya charged her a very expensive $700 to assist with this process. After a long wait, she received the I-20 from the Denver language school. Because there was no US embassy in Libya, she made an appointment for March with the US Embassy in Tunisia to be interviewed for the student visa. As the appointment date approached, so did the fighting. In early March, bombing raids came closer to home. In Zawiyah, fewer than two hours from Tarhuna, a small revolt was quickly crushed by Qaddafi's forces. That early defeat made many Libyans in the east reluctant to oppose Qaddafi. On March 19, NATO started bombing Libya under the jurisdiction of a no-fly zone over the country. This halted Qaddafi's military advance. Although travel was dangerous, the family boarded a flight for their next-door neighbor, Tunisia. After a thorough vetting at the US embassy there, she and the baby were approved, but Sami's situation required further consideration and time.

"I was very upset when they told us that," she said. "We returned home and kept checking with the embassy in Tunisia to see if he had been approved. I was told over and over that it was still in process." During this time, Qaddafi's forces had surrounded the seaside town of Misrata, just miles from Eman and Sami's home. The whole area suffered from scarce food and water, little to no electricity, and a severe shortage of medical supplies. Rebel forces began bombing Misrata in late April, targeting Qaddafi's tanks and artillery. On May 15, they declared the battle for Misrata over.

It had been two months and still no answer from the embassy in Tunisia. Eman and Sami decided on a back-up plan. They would apply for a student visa for her study in Turkey. They received the I-20 from a Turkish language school at the same time that Sami's visa was approved in Tunisia. Excitement and relief came together reassuring them that the US was the right decision. The situation in Libya was becoming worse. "This was our escape," Eman said. Another quick flight to Tunisia to get the student visa stamped for the US meant that a huge hurdle had been crossed but not the last one.

To prepare for their "great adventure," as Eman called it, she went to the internet, the only source of information she trusted. She reviewed online forums posted by Arabic-speaking students who were studying or had studied in the United States. The information she garnered about Colorado stated "it was cold and snowy with little sunshine." Based on this weather report, she started buying clothing for near arctic conditions.

"You can't imagine how much money I spent buying heavy, woolen clothing for all three of us," she said.

The I-20 document for the Denver language school was dated March 15, 2013, but it had taken so long to get Sami's visa approval that this date had passed. They postponed the trip until June and requested a new I-20, which had to come through Dubai in the United Arab Emirates as arranged by the travel agency for another $100. Airline tickets were booked, so the family would arrive just three days before classes in Denver began. The day of the British Airways flight scheduled for 12 noon finally arrived, but at 9 a.m., Eman was still at home repeatedly calling the travel agent to see if the necessary packet had come from Dubai. The stress was just too much.

On the verge of tears, she said, "I'm not going. I give up. We won't be allowed to enter the US without a valid I-20."

Her brother arrived at the house and took the phone from her hand. "You're going right now to the airport." A friend who had studied in the US had told him that the original I-20 would be accepted. Eman, Sami, and 10-month old Saif were hustled into his car along with numerous bags, a backpack, and a stroller.

As they struggled with the bags and approached the ticket counter, the plane was already boarding. "We have to weigh the bags," her brother said. He shook his head in disbelief as he placed the first bag on the scale.

"What is all of this? A prayer rug? Why? A year's supply of diapers? Wipes? Where are you going? To Saturn?"

Clothes were flying every which way as Eman and her brother sorted and emptied bags, leaving many items behind. The ticket clerk leaned over the counter to remind them that the plane could not wait much longer. A throng of family and friends were cheering them on in the background.

They hastily boarded the British Airways plane. A shared "We finally made it!" accompanied their sighs of relief as they settled into their seats. Eman's backpack with their heavy coats, documents, and diaper bags was stashed under her seat. A cousin had suggested Sami should have a backpack, too, but Sami said people would make fun of him because it wasn't acceptable for a man to carry a bag on his back. As Eman looked out the window at the blue curve of the Mediterranean and the ships in the Tripoli harbor, she realized she had achieved a goal but had a larger task piling up on her shoulders along with the heavy backpack. She was the one who was in charge of the travel, the settling-in process, and the tasks of daily living. She was the one who spoke some English, the one on scholarship.

When they arrived at Heathrow in London, they had to spend the night in a hotel before boarding another plane for Chicago. They picked up the stroller and three heavy bags. When they put Saif in the stroller, they discovered it had a broken wheel. "I didn't know what to do," she said. "Sami was carrying bags. I had my backpack and another bag plus the stroller with Saif in it, so I just kept walking side to side."

Even though the British English she heard in Heathrow was confusing, Eman managed to get the family through customs and find a taxi to get them to a hotel for a one-night stay before completion of the trip to America. By the time they arrived at the hotel, they were hungry, thirsty, and ready to cry along with a whimpering Saif, whose bottles of milk had been confiscated in Tripoli when they boarded the plane. They ordered a room service cheese pizza because they were afraid other food might contain pork. The water that came with the order was the "fizzy kind," not what they wanted.

The next lap of their adventure was flying to Chicago. "Let's just throw away the stroller, leave it in the airport," Eman suggested. Seven hours later, they were in the Chicago airport, and guess what? The broken stroller was waiting for them. "Lucky me," she laughed. "I didn't have to carry the baby, but I needed to again walk like a handicapped person." That moment of humor was soon dispelled by a wave of fear when they saw several policemen with dogs weaving through the crowd of travelers heading for passport control. The passport officer quickly reviewed their passports and, although noting that Eman's I-20 was for an earlier date, scanned and accepted it. Another officer stepped up to take them into a small room where they were detained for more than three hours. Eman was asked to move back her head scarf to show her forehead for an official photo. Then it was Sami's turn to be thoroughly questioned. Eman had to translate with the help of her Arabic-English dictionary. He was asked about his occupation, army service, participation in revolutionary activities, and his purpose in coming to the US. Saif was in tears of fatigue and frustration, and his parents were exhausted by the time the interview was finished and they were approved. It was prayer time, so Eman produced two prayer rugs out of her bottomless backpack, and they went to the prayer room in the airport. Then Sami called a contact in Texas who, in turn, called a Libyan student in Denver to meet them.

It was a warm May afternoon in the annex building of Spring International. Eman and I were sitting in the quiet of the empty school director's office because she needed to be near the reception desk to help students during the break between classes. We had left the door open a crack, so she could see the reception area. Just recounting their tedious journey to the US seemed to have exhausted her, but she was also enjoying the humor of looking back at their antics. She wiped her forehead and adjusted her glasses.

"I don't know how you managed," I said. "Saif was only 10 months old, and a very active kid judging from what I've seen of him now." She laughed and reached into a pocket for her smart phone. She quickly found a video of her now four-year-old preschool graduate dressed in a small blue cap and gown. When it came time for him to be in the spotlight, his teacher asked him what he wanted to be when he grew up. He shouted, "I want to be a police!" I was amazed at the transformation from a fatigued toddler on their journey to America and this lively, English-speaking preschooler. "Big plane. Fly" remains his only memory of this complicated journey.

Exhaustion mixed with apprehension was their companion as they exited the off-ramp at Denver International Airport in the Mile High City at 9 p.m. on June 21, 2013. Sami helped Eman hoist her backpack over her shoulders while she grasped the diaper bag in one hand and the dictionary in her other hand. Saif bounced along in his dad's arms as they blindly followed their fellow travelers down an escalator and onto a train that they hoped would take them to baggage claim. Worries abounded. What if the bags weren't there? Without all of their woolen clothes, they would freeze in the Colorado cold. Where would they go if the Libyan student didn't meet them? Would they be able to find a place to stay? They had just three days before their English program would begin. How could they find a baby sitter for Saif?

Eman heard a recorded voice say, "Baggage claim next stop." They followed a white-haired lady who had been on the plane with them and arrived at a carousel to wait for their bags. A short, smiling man approached them.

"Are you Sami?" he asked. "I'm Khaled. Welcome to Colorado."

"*Alhamdulillah*, thanks be to God! We finally have a friend to help us," Eman murmured. Khaled grabbed two bags and walked the family out the doors into his car and then to an apartment where they could stay a few days. What a wonderful feeling to have beds to sleep in, a shower, and even some food in the kitchen! The family's relief turned into a sound night's sleep. The bright Colorado sunshine woke up Eman. She went to the kitchen to find the milk, coffee, bread, and cheese Khaled had left for them. "Eat something to keep your hunger silent," she repeated to herself. Then she opened the balcony doors and stepped outside. It was a warm June morning with the Rocky Mountains framed in the distance against a vivid blue sky.

She looked all around with amazement. "Where is all the snow?"

CHAPTER 7

Tears and Transcripts

LIFE BEGAN IN EARNEST. With Khaled's help, they found a one-bedroom apartment within walking distance of the ESL program that provided their I-20 document. Buying a car was six months into the future, so all of their grocery shopping, errands, and exploration of the city were accomplished on public buses. A Moroccan neighbor babysat Saif during the school day. After three weeks of study, the school informed them that Sami could no longer study because funding for spouses had been discontinued by the Libyan government due to the revolution. They had expected to receive funds for Sami to study English for one year, so he and Eman would take classes together with a hired babysitter for Saif. This was a huge disappointment to Eman, but Sami took it in stride for two reasons. He hadn't had the opportunity to study any English in Libya, not even the alphabet, so even the basic ESL class was too advanced for him. He also realized that his support of Eman's goal of a master's degree would improve their lives in the future. The best way to support her was by being a stay-at-home dad for his son, a task he relished.

"When I look back on this time, I really appreciate that he accepted this change in his life and am thankful for all the help he has given me," Eman said. This role reversal is not easy for an American,

169

let alone for a Libyan husband. Evidently, some Libyans in the same situation continuously complained about their wives and blamed them for all the glitches of living in a new culture.

Eman and Sami were not alone. They were two of approximately 1,343 Libyan students on government scholarships at universities and English language schools in the United States and 500 in Canada in the 2013-2014 academic year, according to the 2013 *Open Doors Report on International Educational Exchange* data. The Libyan Committee for Higher Education began its overseas scholarship program in 2007 when they sent more than 7000 graduate students to other countries. During the civil war and immediately after the overthrow of the Qaddafi regime, funding was on shaky ground, but the transitional government resumed payments just in time for Eman to utilize her scholarship in 2013.

As her English classes progressed throughout the six-week term, she became impatient. The clock of financial support was ticking, and she felt that the classes did not challenge her enough to reach her goal of graduate study. The barrier set by the Libyan scholarship authorities provided financial support for only six months of English and then two years for the master's degree. She knew that they would not have enough of their own money to finance study beyond these time restrictions. "I started to look for another language school that would provide more academic instruction, and through recommendations from friends, I transferred to Spring International at the end of the term." This was a decision that benefited both Spring and Eman.

Eman was a star student from the first day of orientation in October to the day she completed her course of study in March of 2014. Her teachers loved her because she was so likable and motivated. One of her instructors said, "She was a perfect role model for younger students who sometimes saw their time in the US as a vacation." She quickly made friends with Tarfah, a fellow student from Saudi

Arabia, who also had one child, and was working toward the goal of a master's degree and a PhD in early childhood education. The two women became acquainted in the advanced intermediate English class. "We were the only women in a class of all male students and soon discovered we were the only ones who made 100 percent on all the tests." she remembered. They had fun competing for grades, talking together about their families, and sharing their plans for the future. When the instructor Karyl arrived early for the first class of the day, Eman and Tarfah would be studying together in the classroom. Miss Karyl said, "The more responsibilities you two have, the more responsible you are."

When Eman looks back on those responsibilities, they seemed very light because she was filled with the excitement of new experiences in a new country. "We had enough money, lots of energy, and very few of the social obligations that took our time in Libya," she said. As I listened to her describe a typical day during this early part of her life in Colorado, I was overwhelmed by the amount of energy expended just to get to her English classes. "Sami and Saif were still sleeping when I woke up at 7 a.m., ate breakfast, and got ready for school. I walked about four blocks to the Parker RTD station where I took a train to the downtown Denver station, waited about 15 minutes, and took another train to the Littleton station near the school. When school ended, my husband and Saif would be waiting in the car to take me home where I would fix a snack. About 5 p.m., we would take Saif in his stroller or riding his tricycle for a walk around a lake near our apartment. Then we'd shop if necessary, return home where I'd make dinner at 7:30 or 8, watch TV and do homework, and go to bed."

Soon after graduation from Spring International, Eman received a conditional acceptance to graduate school at the University of Colorado Denver; however, the university required a passing score on the International English Language Testing Service (IELTS) exam, one of the major English-language tests in the world for non-native English language speakers. After preparing for the test, she passed it with high score and was fully admitted to university. A major step had been accomplished.

Eman and I were settled back in the conference room at 1 p.m. on a wintry January day. Tempting us on the table was a plate of brownies from the noon-time Conversation Partner get-together for the students and American volunteers. Even though it was her lunch hour, we decided to jump into the pros and cons of her first two years in the United States and wait a few minutes to have a treat. I began the conversation by complimenting her achievements in language proficiency and admission to the university during that time. She thanked me but shook her head. "I was so happy to be at the point of going to graduate school, but I was also very sad and lonely." Eman was homesick for her family in Libya, and keeping in touch was almost impossible because of the chaos of the revolution and the lack of money to make phone calls. They could only afford $40 to $50 a month for calling cards that provided only four minutes for each dollar. Calls had to be made to both Sami's and her relatives, and sometimes they didn't even pick up the calls. "I made a schedule to call my mom every Friday, but first I had to call my sister, who transferred the call to my mother. Sometimes this worked, and sometimes it didn't." Another irritation making adjustment to the US difficult occurred in every phone call Sami made to his family. He was besieged with requests from his father to return to Libya, and of course, his father had great authority in his son's life. "We need you. When are you coming home?" was a recurring question.

"There were many nights when I was so homesick I couldn't sleep and just went out to the apartment balcony and stared at the sky," she recalled. The first year we were here, I felt like a dead person in the grave with only a small hole where I could see people at home and what they were doing. The second year, it seemed like the nerves in my body were frozen. I just didn't care. I asked myself why the family didn't call me to see how I was. I felt like they had forgotten me." Eman had never lived away from her small town in Libya, and although she tired of the continual social obligations, they were a ritualized part of her life. Her family was a magnet that pulled her close and didn't allow her to stray far from them. Now here she was in Denver, Colorado, 6,000 miles away from Al Khadra, Libya. The distance and differences in culture and landscape added to her homesickness.

Her yearning for the close ties of her family was partly due, I perceived, to a major difference in our two cultures. Libya is a collectivist culture where relationships within the family, clan, and tribe emphasize the interconnectedness between people. The United States is more individualistic. We strive for independence, and self-reliance based on a social theory that favors freedom of action. My experience in Egypt and the many years associating with students from the Arab Gulf clarifies the differences in loyalty between these countries and the West. In general, people in collectivist cultures consider themselves to be loyal members of a family group demonstrated by feelings of mutual obligation, commitment, and closeness among family members. An individual's reputation is based on that loyalty, and the family's reputation resides in the female members' virtue. In the US, duty to self usually comes before duty to family or friends. Student comments in a semantic differential survey I conducted with Saudi students several years earlier put a face on these differences: "Relationships of Americans are weak." "Family is not as important to Americans." "Our people love to work cooperatively and communicate with each other. Americans work alone" "American women need to think about their bad reputations," and "American families kick their children out of the house when they turn eighteen." The shock and resulting loneliness that Eman was experiencing grew out of the contrasts between our cultures.

I paused the recorder, so we could sample the brownies on the table. While we nibbled, Eman asked, "Weren't you just as homesick in Egypt?" I told her that I missed my parents and my friends but thought it was easier for me because I had already lived away from home when I went to university. My first step toward independent living was just a small one: sixty-five miles away to live in a university dormitory. Then in our senior year, my husband and I were married, earning enough money as editors of the college newspaper to live without help from our parents. After we graduated, we moved to Columbia, Missouri, where my husband began studying for a master's degree in journalism while I taught English in middle school. I missed my mom and dad, but it was easy to call them, write letters, or visit during our two years there. After several moves, advanced degrees, and three children, we signed up for our first cross-cultural experience at American University in Cairo, Egypt. By this time, we had established homes in many places.

Eman had never experienced life away from home until she came to Colorado. It left a huge hole in her heart. She tried to fill the loneliness with hard work toward her goal of higher education. As was true of Nisren's and Raad's married life in the United States, Eman's relationship with Sami had changed since they arrived here. "Even though we'd been married three years, I didn't really know my husband until we came here," she said. "At home, we both were so busy: he with his job at the press and I with my social schedule and pressure from relatives. My experience here helped me to understand Sami more and to understand myself, too."

In Libya, her time was never her own. It was scheduled by her family, her work, and her study. In the US, she discovered she could spend her free time, although it was limited, in ways she chose, including personal time with Sami and Saif. Along with more independence, she was pleasantly surprised at the acceptance she found for her Muslim identity. "When I took the bus and train and went to class, everyone was so friendly, even friendlier than some of my fellow Muslims," she said. However, the family couldn't avoid the inevitable shock of living in such a new environment. Culturally, the first jolt was seeing men and women kissing in the airport. Expressions of affection were never allowed in public in Libya. Then everywhere they looked, they saw differences in the mix of people: varied skin colors and nationalities, women's dress from conservative to almost naked, religious buildings of different faiths. At home in Libya, there was a sameness that was dependable, but here it was difficult to know how to react to and how to interface with the differences.

"In Libya, we had very few people from other cultures or religions. There were a few churches and some Ukrainian and European nurses and doctors but not much diversity. I realize now that I have become more open to people of other cultures and religions, and I enjoy that," she explained.

One neighborly experience especially underscored some cultural differences. A woman who lived in the apartment house had asked Eman where she was from and what language she spoke. She seemed enthusiastic about getting acquainted. "I have a friend who speaks Arabic," she told her. "Could we visit you sometime?" In her always friendly manner, Eman replied, "Of course, you can." At 9 p.m. on the following Sunday, she was straightening up the kitchen after putting Saif to bed. She was eager to have some time for herself when she heard a knock on her door. She opened it to find the neighbor and an African-American woman.

Hospitality was ingrained in Eman, so she welcomed them and opened the door wide.

When the two women were settled on the sofa, she offered to bring them some soft drinks or orange juice. They politely refused as they busily pulled pamphlets and a Bible from a briefcase.

"This Bible is a gift for you. It's translated into Arabic," the neighbor woman said in English sprinkled with a few Arabic phrases.

Eman had been offered the Bible and many pamphlets on other occasions, so she understood that the two women were trying to convert her to Christianity. They asked her if she had questions. She paused, considering whether or not to list the questions she had asked of other people. She was tired and eager to finish the visit, so she hastily offered her most common concerns: Do you believe Jesus is God? Do you have three separate gods: Son, Holy Spirit, and God? Why do you have so many versions of the Bible? Can just anyone translate it?

The two women sat back on the sofa and looked at each other with the hope that one of them would have adequate answers. Although they had received some training from their church, they struggled to respond. After fifteen minutes, the conversation dwindled. Hoping to add a final word that would set her beliefs in a context the visitors might understand, she said, "In Islam, we have many prophets, Adam, Essa (Jesus), and Muhammad, who was the last prophet, the one who brought us the true words of the Koran."

The women didn't encourage her to continue but asked if they could pray for her. She politely agreed and thanked them for coming.

Eman remembers the exact date. It was August 21, 2013. She was excited about graduate student orientation and a meeting with her advisor. She traveled by light rail to the University of Colorado Denver, a 150-acre downtown campus that included three institutions: CU-Denver, Metropolitan State University, and Community College of Denver. This sprawling campus was a far-cry from her small, close-knit institutions of higher education in Libya. Nearly 42,000 students and 5,000 faculty and staff comprise the collective campus population. This could have been a daunting experience for her, but instead she found it exciting and energizing. After she located the right building and the large orientation hall, she joined a long line of students. Although she knew no one in the line, she was smiling and approachable. A pretty woman wearing a hijab, black pants, and a fashionable Burberry scarf over her long shirt, smiled back. They moved together in the line and began talking. This casual conversation developed into a close friendship that played a huge part in Eman's life. Her new friend was Neena, a Saudi woman studying for her doctorate.

"Now whenever I'm depressed, I call Neena. She takes me to Starbuck's for a caramel cappuccino, and I tell her everything," Eman told me.

Unfortunately, Neena could not accompany Eman into the office of her graduate advisor. "I was very happy and excited to meet my advisor," she said. "He seemed like a nice gentleman until he began laughing at my background."

"Oh, look at this! What is this?" the professor laughed as he perused her official transcript from the University in Libya. "Why all the stamps?"

"This is how it works in my country. It must be approved by the registrar and the dean and certified by an official translator. Then I had to go to the Ministry of Foreign Affairs to get the final stamp," she explained.

He opened his eyes wide and shook his head in amazement.

"What kind of operating systems and programs have you worked with?"

At this point, Eman was feeling defensive but also deficient. She explained that MS-DOS was the main system she used, that she had taught programming to her fellow students, and that she was at CU-Denver "to refresh her information and follow the trends of modern technology," a phrase she had rehearsed before meeting the professor.

He scoffed again. "Your transcript of classes in Libya is ten years old. I can't even show it to the committee. You'll need to take four undergrad courses the first two semesters and pass with an A or B."

Eman responded by requesting an adjustment in the requirements because she had taken two of the classes in Libya. The answer was "No." The interview was abruptly over.

As she left the campus to take the bus home, she steeled herself to face an additional obstacle. The CBIE would not pay for undergraduate courses unless they were mixed with graduate requirements, and the time limit of her study was only two years. She didn't have time to take prerequisites. The first semester, she enrolled in two graduate classes and one undergrad class, Discreet Structure, a course that required advanced mathematics.

"The first day in that class, I couldn't understand the professor's math vocabulary. I felt like I was lost in a new world of information that I couldn't navigate. I actually got a zero on the first quiz and considered leaving to study in Turkey, where you never hear of anyone failing a class."

Although Eman was passing the two graduate classes, she cried almost every day. "I missed the deadline to drop the math class and was supposed to pay back the tuition to CBIE with money I didn't have." The agency finally released her from repayment, and she dropped the class but took it her third semester from a different professor who simplified the explanations and graded on the curve.

Neena and an Indian friend who was a graduate student gave her advice about three courses to take second semester. By then, she was more confident, and student life was settling down. Sami was taking good care of Saif, and Eman was multitasking studies with mothering and housewifely duties. Because she had been in the US for two years, her scholarship fund, which was more regularized now, included payment for a trip home. She and Sami were so excited at being able to see their families that they began planning months in advance, a necessity because a tangle of red tape was required. She called the CBIE in Canada to freeze her scholarship money for the two months they would spend in Libya. The agency then had to contact the Libyan Ministry for approval. This lengthy process wasn't finished by the time the family was to travel, so they used money they had saved for the trip with the promise that it would be refunded after their return.

"Wait a minute," I interrupted. "How in the world did you save money on your small monthly allotment?"

"I'm a great saver," she exclaimed, rapidly citing the figures from their monthly budget. "We were paid $2,500, and our apartment was $1,200; utilities about $200 or less; car insurance, $100, and food about $600 a month for the three of us. I was able to save about $500 a month."

Libyan scholars did not have the luxury of the salaries received by Arab students on scholarship from the Gulf countries of Qatar, United Arab Emirates, and Saudi Arabia. Their monthly allotments were almost double that of the Libyans in addition to paid trips home every year. When money was scarce for the Libyan community, the Libyan students stepped forward to help each other. If monthly salaries did not arrive on time or were simply cut off, students borrowed money from their friends. "When they saw that we were not in need, they would ask us for a loan and then offer to help us when necessary. Usually the money was paid back on a deadline, but once in a while when we asked for help, our friends wouldn't even take our phone calls."

As the family made preparations for their trip home, Eman considered the worst case scenario of not being allowed to return to the United States. She decided to put all of their furniture in storage and move out of the apartment. During her third semester, two months in advance of the necessary visa interview at the American Embassy in Istanbul, their plans were tested by a surprising revelation. Eman found out she was pregnant.

"I had no option to postpone the trip, so I just asked Allah to keep the baby safe."

CHAPTER 8

Reverse Culture Shock

It was the end of final week at Spring International with the stress on office staff of grade reports, tallying absences, planning graduation, and student questions about next term. Eman took time after finishing her tasks to meet with me in the quiet of an unused classroom. She was always calm, smiling, and eager to talk. The focus of our interview was her trip back to Libya. I told Eman about Nisren's travel to Baghdad. The two women hadn't had the opportunity to meet yet, but I had shared some of their common experiences with each of them.

"Both of you were disappointed in your trips back home," I said, "but you had the added discomfort of morning sickness and extreme heat in July."

Eman responded with a deep sigh. "Not only was I sick, but I was disgusted with what I saw. The sand, the dirt, bombed-out buildings, and roads with no traffic signals, just checkpoints where our bags and cars were inspected. I didn't expect to see trash almost everywhere and had forgotten what it was like to have no air conditioning and lack of water."

It was also during Ramadan, so there was fasting from sunrise to sundown. An hour's drive to Misrata proved to be "a shopping trip from hell." She walked into a shopping center to buy some traditional clothes she couldn't find in the US and discovered sand in the shops, clothes piled everywhere, no price tags, and no way to return something because there were no receipts. Thoughts of Wal-Mart displays and organization provided a stark contrast. Her quick smile turned into a frown of disbelief. "It was a shock, but it was home and family. It's what I had wanted so much and waited for."

I mentioned the idea of reverse culture shock, the psychological, emotional, and cultural re-entrance into your own culture. She recognized the term and its application to her experience. "It seemed like everything had changed, and no one was really interested in talking about our lives in the United States. We felt the American experience was helping us to succeed in our goals, but there was a jealousy among our friends and family. Some people in our part of the world, Eastern people, fight the success of others; most Western people encourage that success."

"A good part of this is that you've changed, isn't it?" I asked.

She considered the possible changes in herself. We talked about living abroad and how she had adapted to American culture and had adjusted her attitudes, feelings, and even the relationships with her country and her family. This time, she did smile and leaned forward to say, "You know what I've learned? Coming to the US was my golden opportunity. I've discovered myself more and widened my vision of the world itself." Several times in past conversations, Eman said she wanted to return to Libya at some point to work and contribute to rebuilding the country. Her visit pasted some reality on what life would be like if this actually happened.

"I can't imagine going back to all that mess," she said. "I would lose everything. How would I manage my life? How would we live? I would probably have to stay home and make do with tutoring students and do some little businesses, like selling almonds. If the university was still functioning, I could be an assistant professor, but I wouldn't earn real money, just an amount in my bank account, no cash. People sleep at the banks at night to get money in the morning."

She showed me a video clip on her phone of a long line at a bank. A man in military uniform pushed and hit a woman to get in the front of the line.

"If we were there now, my kids would probably go to public school because private schools are too expensive, and they wouldn't get a good education. They would lose the English they've learned." On weekends, Saif was enrolled in an Arabic language school at a Denver mosque, so he was learning his native language along with English.

One of the worst fears of a return to Libya was the possibility of kidnapping. "People think you're rich if you've lived in the United States, and that makes you a target." She cited the recent abduction of a doctor whose family was asked to pay 400,000 dinars for his release. The family collected the money for the militia, got his release, and then he was kidnapped again with the demand for more money or death. Even university professors had been threatened if they did not pay a bribe.

Just as in Nisren's case, Eman's family had become accustomed to the daily threats and the discomforts of life. Returning home seemed plausible to some of the relatives. "My family is used to their lives in the middle of chaos. They just don't understand the differences between life in a free, stable country and life there."

She quickly launched into a list of the changes she hoped her country would someday experience. "I would like Libyan kids to learn how to organize their lives, even in a simple way, like forming a line when you're waiting. We also need to teach confidence, presentation skills, and the ability to ask questions in class. I would also have buses everywhere with certain schedules, so you don't have to rely on someone to drive. Recycling is a new idea. We throw away everything." Her wish list also included a respect for time and timeliness. "When Libyans have a party at 5 p.m., guests come at 7. Workers don't arrive on time because they know they will be paid anyway. Businesses should have regularized hours. My mom and dad taught us to be organized. I like to plan ahead. Going back to Libya would be like going back in time. I'm also used to being in charge here in the US. At home, I would sit on the porch and look at the clouds, and Sami would spend the whole day with his brothers."

What American cultural traits would Eman leave out of her bags if she went home? Lack of neighborliness loomed largest. "My next door neighbors don't know if I'm alive or dead," she laughed. "People don't seem to have strong relationships with each other. Parents allow teens to leave home when they turn eighteen. Sometimes I see old ladies who don't have anyone to help them. My neighbor told me she was going to have a knee replacement, but her daughter told her she couldn't help because she had her own life."

Eman returned from Libya in August, just in time for her fourth semester of university study with one more to go. It wasn't an easy semester for a student in in the fifth, sixth, and seventh months of pregnancy. She had one undergraduate class and two graduate level courses. It also was the last semester of her scholarship. She applied for an extension with the Libyan Ministry but was refused. Sami asserted himself and told her to take three classes, so she could finish as much as possible before the money ran out.

"How am I going to deliver a baby and complete three courses?" she responded. But the ever-present mantra of "Swallow it now..." nudged her along. Some of the class projects required nighttime meetings, so on those days, she would remain on campus from mid-morning to 7 p.m. Christmas vacation provided no respite because she was completing a project for one of the previous fall classes. Exhausted and just a few weeks from delivery, she returned to a new semester the third week in January. She knew that her scheduled C-section was January 28th or 29th, so she had to ask her professors if they would allow her to make up two weeks of class assignments while she was recuperating. When she went to make the request to one of her toughest professors, he cut her off in mid-sentence. "Just don't bother taking my class. That's the simplest way." Another professor, who was Iranian, gave her permission to be absent for two weeks as long as she completed work on a group project. An Indian friend in the class put Eman into a group with other Indian students, so they could help her. Any cultural barriers that might have existed disappeared when the international graduate students were all striving for the same goal. They worked beautifully as a team supporting each other.

Baby Sanad was born on January 20, 2015, at Swedish Hospital. Eman's five days in the hospital were the most restful of many months. "It was a great experience for me with a wonderful nurse who actually came and took the baby so I could sleep, very different from my hospital stay with Saif's birth." Although Sami didn't actually see the birth because the sight of blood made him nauseous, he comforted her at the head of the surgery table and enjoyed the whole process. Neena came to support Eman. She was elected to cut the baby's cord, an action that might have caused Sami to faint. When Sami had his first opportunity to hold the baby, he whispered the Islamic call to prayer in each ear, a traditional way of welcoming this gift of God.

When they took the baby home, Sami's duties as a stay-at-home father expanded to include feeding, diaper changes, laundry, and all the tasks that went with caring for a newborn. "My husband really became the mother and father to Sanad. I never would have expected to see him holding an infant and giving him formula," Eman said.

"This is my son," Sami said, "even though I didn't give birth to him."

A sick-leave letter from the hospital gave her two more weeks to stay home with her new son. Because of excessive bleeding, she was told to rest several more days. "I was in pain and busy with my little boy when my Indian friend called and said our project report was due the next day. I asked the professor if I could be excused, and he said 'No.'"

Eman was worried that Sami wouldn't be able to care for a newborn baby while she was busy in graduate school. In a call home, her sister advised, "Just teach him, and then leave him alone." She took the advice by giving her husband a lesson in baby care before her first day back. And it worked! However, she did call Sami from campus almost hourly to ask how the baby was doing. She discovered that her husband was an even better nursemaid than she would have been.

I could picture Eman, with her laptop in her backpack, waiting at the bus stop in freezing temperatures in February because Sami had to stay with the baby. She had never learned to drive, and even if she had, they didn't have money for a second car. Sometimes she felt physically unable to take another step, but she persevered. A group project with her Indian friends required many extra meetings, but they understood her condition and gave her extra help. When final exam time arrived, she had used up all the energy she possessed.

"My brain was frozen. I left blank pages in the test and watched the Google timer tick, ticking on the big screen in the classroom. When the time was up, I started crying. I got the worst grade of my life," she admitted. During spring break, I cried every day." When she returned to school to explain her situation to the Iranian professor, he said that grades on her assignments were good, but she had received a failing grade on the final exam.

"You're Muslim, aren't you?" he said. "You know that in Islam it's not fair to help some people and not the others."

"I wasn't asking for favors," Eman said. "I was just explaining."

He told her he would consider her case and let her know. It took some bravery, but Eman went to the department chair to see if there was a solution for her problem. The chair told her that there was an option for her, a grade of Incomplete. Because she had a medical reason, she could make up the final. Eman was greatly relieved. When she returned to class, the professor had changed his mind and told the entire group that he had curved the grades. She had passed.

In March of 2015, just three months after Eman had given birth, she received an email from the CBIE. A bureau spokeswoman wrote, "Program funding has been delayed several times in the past year, and the program currently lacks funds to cover students' essential benefits, including living allowances, health insurance and tuition fees." Chaos in Libya was the cause of fluctuations in student benefits. Since Eman and Sami had left their country, a first civil war had erupted, followed by foreign military intervention, the ousting and death of Qaddafi, and the proliferation of armed groups that led to violence and instability. A second civil war had begun earlier this year causing oil output to plunge. Oil fields, export terminals and revenues from existing sales became prizes for the many warring factions, including the Islamic State. Payments to US universities and ESL programs were usually late and sometimes did not arrive at all.

Then in May, universities and ESL programs did not receive tuition payments, and students were unable to pay rent and other living expenses. Many Libyan students had to depend on the kindness of their institutions to put tuition payments on hold and on landlords who would let them pay their rent in a lump sum when, and if, stipends came through. "These are really first-class students," said John Sunnygard, executive director of the Office of International

Affairs at the University of Colorado Denver, which had twenty-six Libyan scholarship students, including Eman. "It's very painful to see the impact that events far away have on students and their families. This is the next generation of Libyans. They are the ones who will rebuild Libya. We take that responsibility very seriously." The next drop in a roller coaster year came in July.

The time allowed for her scholarship was finished. She asked for a one-semester extension, but her request was rejected, and she was told she would have to pay for the three remaining courses toward her master's degree. She later discovered she probably would have gotten the extension except for the fact that someone in Libya had taken her name off the scholarship list before it came to the CBIE. The Foreign Student Advisor at the university said she would have to terminate her visa unless she could provide a bank statement that guaranteed that she had enough money for her last semester's tuition of $5000. She applied for economic hardship, a visa option that would authorize employment for F-1 students. This category covered severe economic hardship caused by unforeseen circumstances, such as a loss of financial aid or on-campus employment, fluctuations in the value of currency or exchange rate, inordinate increases in tuition and /or living costs, unexpected changes in the financial condition of the student's source of support, and so on. Her situation fit into the requirements. Permission to work was granted, so she began looking for a job. When prospective employers saw her class schedule, they found it impossible to fit work hours into it. If there was no work, how could they get the tuition money for next semester and still have enough to live on? They had saved some money by moving to a cheaper apartment in subsidized housing. Sami found some resources although he couldn't legally work. They borrowed money from friends, and Eman's brother in Libya managed to send a small amount. It was still not enough.

One of her former teachers at Spring International met her for lunch one day and found out about the possibility that she would lose her student status and be sent home to Libya. She contacted the director at Spring, who offered Eman a part-time job as an office assistant three days a week. It was just enough money for the family to put food on the table and possibly to pay rent but not enough to guarantee that her tuition would be paid. Only one solution remained. Sami would ask a friend to put some money in their bank account, so they could get a statement for the university and then return the money to him.

This wasn't the final maneuver in the obstacle course. With her last semester guaranteed, she had to think ahead to what would happen when she graduated. Her student visa would run out when she stopped studying, which meant she would have to go home to Libya within 30 days of graduating. There were only two options. One was returning to Libya. Although she desperately wanted to visit her family and introduce them to the one-year-old they had never seen, she did not want to permanently return. She and Sami were afraid to take their two young sons to a country where the Islamic State was active, where detentions, kidnappings, and torture happened daily, where killings occurred in your own back alleyway, and where you didn't know who was for you or against you. There was no stable government, no assurance of services, and no adequate medical care.

"There would be no opportunity to practice what I had learned at a decent salary. So why did I get the degree? Here there is hope, education for our sons, safety, and freedom," she said.

The second option, which was only a temporary solution, was Optional Practical Training (OPT) for international students. It was a United States Citizenship and Immigration Services (USCIS) category that would allow her, as an F-1 student, to take a job that was directly related to her computer science degree for up to twelve months. At least twenty hours per week were required for this option, for which they could be paid or could volunteer as interns. It would take ninety days or more to process an application before graduation. A fee of $410 triggered the process. Now she had to find a position that would fulfill the requirements for her OPT.

In the midst of a frantic search for an employer, the dream of a lifetime became a reality. On May 14, 2016, Eman covered her long tan dress with a black graduation robe highlighted by a yellow hood. She carefully fastened the black mortar board on top of her hijab and marched proudly across the stage to get her Master's of Science diploma in computer science. She was thrilled to shake the hand of the president of the University of Colorado at Denver. Graduation was a lifetime award after a childhood of herding sheep and struggling to get an education in a culture that favored men above women. In the audience were her husband, her sons, and three teachers from Spring International.

"Sami felt like he was the one graduating. After I received the diploma, I kissed his forehead and said, 'This is yours, not mine.'"

Her gratitude cut a wide swath to reach across the miles to her Libyan family. "I felt so thankful for my parents and my grandmother and for every member of my family, and I pray that Allah will reward them for everything they have done," she said.

CHAPTER 9

You Can't Go Home Again

EMAN APPLIED HER CHARACTERISTIC PERSISTENCE AND ORGANIZATIONAL SKILL TO THE JOB HUNT TO FULFILL HER OPT OBLIGATIONS. But to no avail. Numerous online applications, phone calls, and enrolling with a job search company produced only a few telephone interviews, and none of those merited an in-face meeting with an employer. It was my feeling that the Islamic-sounding name on her resume and her undergraduate degree from Libya were immediate turn-offs for those who might otherwise have hired her. Time was passing, and she had to do something or be sent home to the nightmare of chaos in Libya. Her part-time job at Spring International led to a more computer-centered position with The Denver Language Institute, an ESL program on the sixth floor of an historic building in downtown Denver. She happily accepted this offer but, as always, she had to look toward an uncertain future.

After just a year, when the OPT was completed, she would again be faced with the obligation to return to Libya or find a legal way to stay in the United States. The unrest in Libya had caused many Libyan students in the United States to consider ways to remain here. In one of our interview sessions, Eman told me about a conversation she and Sami had with an immigration attorney regarding asylum.

She knew that other Libyans had seen an immigration attorney who advised them to apply for political asylum even if they didn't qualify for it. He said the process would take several years and give them a legal way of staying in the US even if they were rejected later. I was skeptical about the advice that was given and after doing some online research, found that this specific lawyer had lost his license to practice in another state and had several complaints filed against him. I suggested accompanying Eman to visit a well-respected immigration attorney that had advised other Spring International students over the years. The attorney presented the two options that were available: asylum status or an H-1B visa. He told us that asylum is granted to people who have been persecuted or fear persecution in their country of origin. Because strict documentation of their persecution is required, very few applicants receive this status. The attorney reiterated the extensive backlog for these cases with many applicants waiting for five years or more. If asylum were granted, Eman and her family could apply for a permanent resident card, a green card, one year after the judgment. Sami would legally be able to work during the waiting period, but they could not travel back and forth to Libya.

"Does that mean we couldn't even go for a short visit?" Eman asked.

The attorney told her that would be impossible, but he suggested the other option, the H-1B, a non-immigrant visa that allowed a foreign national to work temporarily in the United States for up to six years. It was renewable every three years if approved by the USCIS. The glitch here was each year only 85,000 H-1Bs are available, with an additional 20,000 awarded to workers that hold a master's degree or higher from an accredited US university. More than 200,000 applicants petitioned in previous years. When an excess of petitions is received during the first five business days allotted for petitions, the agency will use a computer-generated lottery system to randomly select the number of petitions required to meet the cap.

"Could we travel to Libya if I had an H-1B?" was her immediate question. The answer was affirmative. The family could travel home to visit, and as an added advantage, permanent residency was possible under H-1B status. The difficulty, however, was the requirement that she would need an employer to cover the costs which, including an attorney's fee, could range from $3,000 to $6,000. The attorney also told us that there was no time to spare. The deadline for H-1B applications was just one month away. She would have to find a company to hire her and be willing to pay the attorney fee. Again, she would be in competition with Americans who had the same qualifications and who didn't wear hijab and have a Muslim name.

As I drove her home from our attorney session, she voiced the persistent ache for her parents, a sandstorm of homesickness that obscured the possibility of applying for asylum. Her need to see her family was unfathomable to me when I considered the dangers of even visiting Libya for a short time.   I had recently read a Human Rights Report that described conditions in Libya. Armed groups affiliated with different factions were executing persons extra-judicially, attacking civilians and their property, abducting and disappearing people. ISIS-affiliated fighters were still present in the country. Adding to these fears were the thousands of migrants and asylums seekers departing by boat from Libya as they tried to reach Europe by sea. The relatively short distance between Libya's shoreline and Greece or the Italian island of Lampedusa have encouraged migrants from North Africa, the Middle East, and South Asia regions to flee their countries through Libya. This migration directly affected Eman when she received a Facebook message from one of her brothers. He was frustrated and angry about the increasing danger and lack of opportunity for a decent life. He had joined other migrants on a boat to Italy, but the boat had capsized just off the coast. He was one of the few survivors. This didn't deter him. He tried again and had made it to Rome, where he was being processed for resettlement.

The chaos in her country did not affect Eman's desire to travel home. It convinced me that no matter how chaotic and decimated your country is, it remains your identity, and you still miss it and love it. Eman believed that the choice of asylum would not only mean a rejection of her family, but it also would be dishonest. She would have to lie about specific threats to her life because she did not have proof of any personal danger if she returned to Libya.

"You're living on such a limited amount of money," I said. "What about the advantage of Sami being able to work if you applied for asylum?"

"I know we're barely making it each month now, but if I choose asylum, it would be like putting myself in a cage and throwing away the key in the sea. I wouldn't be able to go home to visit. My relationship with family means more than anything. In fact, living abroad and such a long distance away has made me feel the real value of family."

Her thoughts turned to the other option. She would have to find an employer willing to pay the fees necessary to apply for the H-1B, and of course, there was the chance that she would not be one of the 20,000 quota reserved for advanced degree holders. However, if she found a job in her field, it would give her the necessary experience to validate her degree. Besides that, the visa would be valid for three years plus possible renewal for another three. She could visit Libya. However, Sami could not legally work.

Eman's chin was quivering as we drew up to the parking lot near her apartment. Thoughts of the H-1B and loyalty to her family were tugging at her emotions in spite of the practical aspect of the asylum process that would allow Sami to work and provide money to meet their expenses. I reminded her of her visit to Libya when she was pregnant with Saif. She acknowledged the negative feelings she had at that time. "I know that, but I'm desperate to see my mom and dad and my family, and I'm not afraid of the dangers there. If it were possible, I would just take my little one and go back to visit. Of course, I can't travel without my husband, so the whole family would have to go."

Libyan women didn't have the right to travel abroad without permission of a male relative. This religious edict never became a law, but it still existed and could cause problems if she traveled alone.

The clock was ticking, and Eman set in motion an extensive job search. She shared the attorney's information about the H-1B with the administrator of The Denver Language Institute. He agreed to sponsor Eman if she did not find a position with another employer. After Eman's job search produced no results, it was agreed that the Institute would sponsor her. Her unique combination of fluency in Arabic and English enabled her to interface with the many Arabic-speaking students in its student body. Her computer skills also were invaluable in maintaining the school's computer lab and solving technical problems for instructors and students. She hurried to submit the paperwork for her petition and waited two months for the decision to be issued. With great relief, she received the necessary status. The family of four could safely stay in the United States for the next few years but living only on Eman's limited salary because Sami was not legally allowed to work. Not the best of situations. She started planning for a visit to Libya, but politics intervened. Under the new Trump administration, security clearance checks had been imposed on target countries, including Libya. It was likely that they would be subject to extended security checks when they applied for both the entry and the return visas in Turkey, where they might be delayed by the process for as long as two to three months. The visa application might even be rejected, so they would have to return to Libya. Her dream of visiting her parents had been shattered.

Eman easily made the transition from graduate student to employee at the new language center. "I was considered part of the faculty and staff and saw how connected and supportive the teachers were to each other. I got to know many Asian, African, and Latino students and their cultures. The key that opened the good relationship I had with students was remembering each one by his or her name and pronouncing it correctly," she explained.

At first, new students were curious about Eman's conservative dress and her hijab, but once they felt the warmth of her ready smile, they felt comfortable with her and frequently asked for her help. At this point in the school's enrollment, half of the students were Arabic-speaking men and a few women from Middle Eastern countries or Libya. Eman held her own with the male students. She recalled an occasion when she was assisting a class with student evaluations of the program at the end of a term.

One of the young men was a bit lazy and asked a friend to tell him what to write down. The friend said, 'Just ask Eman. She'll do it for you.'"

Eman heard him and replied, "I can help you understand, but I won't do it for you."

"But you're like my sister," the student said.

"I may be like your sister, but I'm also part of the staff of the school, and you need to respect that," she retorted.

Eman saw this experience as a lesson to the young men. "After that, they treated me with respect."

Eman also received respect and interest as a speaker at meetings of several community organizations. I had a request from a local Optimists Club to present a program about Muslim women. Rather than a second-hand presentation from me, I suggested that they meet Eman to hear her story of life in Libya and the United States. She was excited about being asked to talk at a meeting of "people with optimism about life." She confidently stood in front of the group of twenty-five men and women, businesspeople, teachers, and community leaders. Her journey from sheepherding to a university degree framed her story, followed by clear answers to questions about Islam and women. The group's applause and requests to spend more time with her affirmed her success. This presentation led to her addressing a church group of more than fifty adults and teenagers who wanted to know more about Islam and its followers.

Several months had gone by since Eman and I had last talked. At this point, she and her family had been in the United States for almost five years. I went to downtown Denver to visit her at the Institute. As I rounded block after block looking for a parking spot, I thought about how far she had come from an olive orchard in a small village to an office building in a metropolis of almost three million people. We sat across from each other in a small classroom with a view of the snow-tipped mountains. Hanging over her was a palpable aura of sadness. She looked tired, and her smile disappeared quickly.

"I'm stuck," she said. "When I talked to Neena last night, I was filled with negativity. I realized I'd never taken time for myself since I was a little kid. My life was always challenged, and time was never my own, even as a child. For ten years, my education and my jobs were always scheduled around caring for the sheep and pleasing my relatives' social schedule. I even had to schedule the day and time when I could take a shower." She tapped her clenched hand on the desk between us. "My friend told me my life was all about climbing one mountain after another, but now I don't have any energy left."

We talked about the changes in her life in the last year. She still had professional goals for a computer job that challenged her more than what she was doing but had been unable to find that job. Her family had no money to travel to other places in the United States because Sami was unable to work legally. She could not visit her beloved family because of the danger and the possibility that she would be unable to return to the US. At the end of her H-1B time, her only options would be returning to Libya or applying for residency and a green card, which would require an expensive sponsorship by an employer. Then, too, the success of receiving residency was limited by the current climate against immigrants, particularly those from Muslim countries. Added to her downward spiral were the differences between her goals and ambitions and Sami's. Although Eman was very grateful for Sami's acceptance of primary care-giving for their two sons, she had hoped for a more equal partnership during their five-year marriage. Her husband did not feel the need to become proficient in English, so much of the burden for the household was in Eman's hands. In previous conversations, I could see she was having difficulties coping with their differences in child-rearing, personalities, and ways of thinking. "But you know," she said, "my husband has more good traits than I had ever expected." She went on to say that getting to know your future husband before marriage doesn't always make it better because they promise everything to impress you. "Neither one of you shows your real face. The masks come off later."

She looked up at me with a slight smile. "Not to worry," she said. "I don't want these things to stop me from moving forward. Everything comes by chance. Another door will open."

CHAPTER 10

Postscript

It was a crisp September afternoon in downtown Denver. Restaurants on the 16th Street Mall were just starting to clear out as I walked down the street to the building where Eman worked. It had been several months and several drafts since she and I had met. I needed to get an update on her situation and some final thoughts on the process of telling me her life story. After a flurry of emails back and forth, we finally found a time to meet. She had added two night classes to her packed schedule of work and family tasks in the hope that an IT Tech and Support Certificate would enhance her ability to get a higher-paid position. My memory of how dispirited she was during our last interview was triggered by the look of concern on her face when she met me at the entrance to the Institute. We walked by a group of Asian and Latin American students hurrying on their way to the last class of the day. She greeted them and wished them "a relaxing weekend, but don't forget to do your homework." We walked into the empty computer lab where she offered me a chair at the desk in front of the computer stations. As usual, she had planned ahead. A pot of tea and two cups were set out next to a spiral notebook that held the final draft of her part of the book. I complimented her on the green and gold patterned head scarf she was wearing. It emphasized the flecks of gold in her eyes. Her warm smile returned. We settled down at the desk for a cup of tea, a replacement for the lunch she had skipped to do her homework for the night class.

An update about her family came first. Eman was eager to tell me about Sanad and Saif, who were now six and eight years old and just starting kindergarten and second grade. The first day of school was memorable for both boys, who were now in different school buildings in the Cherry Creek School District. As the knowledgeable older brother, Saif accompanied Eman and Sanad to his little brother's new school. Sanad was going to have the same teacher, Miss Kathy, that he had loved last year. Eman pulled the smart phone from the pocket in her long dress to show me a photo of the boys with the teacher. "Miss Kathy saw us at the door to her classroom and hurried out to give Saif a hug," she said. "He was so happy that she remembered him." They were delighted when she invited them into the room that was starting to fill up with five and six year olds. "I have something to show you," the teacher said as she picked up the smart phone on her desk. She scrolled through her photos until she came to one of Eman, Sami, Saif and Sanad she had taken last year on Saif's first day of school. "Only an American teacher would have done such a nice thing," Eman said. When Sanad came home at the end of his first day, he told his dad that he liked his teacher, but "Papa, please change my school. Find a school that has a bus like Saif has."

As Eman and I caught up on her family news, I thought back to the time I had first met her when she was a new student at Spring International's orientation. Her intermediate English had flourished into a near-native accent, formal grammar and extensive vocabulary. I asked about Sanad and Saif's fluency in English. She told me that it took Saif, who was only ten months old when they arrived in the US, more than a year to begin speaking more than a few words in either language. Because he was at home with his dad, who spoke only Arabic, he wasn't exposed to English speakers other than his mom. "Now if he doesn't understand the exact meaning of an English word, he'll say 'Mama, what does that mean in Arabic?' When I tell him, I can see he already knows, but he's just checking up on me." Sanad's English and Arabic have flourished along with his older brother's. He quickly recognizes speakers of either language and adjusts his conversation to match. "With kids at school, the boys think of themselves as Americans, but with Libyans, they act like Libyans. They are a combination of both nationalities," Eman explained. "Even their values are a mixture of both." Like all kids, Saif brings home new words he learns at school and these are quickly repeated by his little brother. Recently Eman heard Sanad refuse to eat something he didn't like with the retort "No shit! I don't like that." He was quickly reprimanded: "We don't say that here, Sanad." She told me that the boys are now old enough to go to the mosque with their father for Friday prayers. The learning curve was sharp for Sanad the first few times. Instead of kneeling with his baba on a prayer rug, he wondered why everyone was in this unusual position on the floor, so he would walk around and peer at each person. His dad scolded him and told him he had to behave like the adults. Now every Friday when all the men are getting up to leave the mosque, Sanad gives his dad the thumbs up sign and says, "Baba, today I was a good boy!"

Baba Sami understands more English now but is still uncomfortable speaking, so Eman must be the go-between for tasks like car repairs, shopping, medical appointments, conversations with neighbors, and the apartment manager. Because of their visa situation, he cannot work legally, so their income is at poverty level for a family of four. Although Eman is an excellent money manager, it makes life difficult as Saif and Sanad grow and their needs grow with them. A new job with better pay would help immensely. Eman tells me that she is considering an application for residency in the US. Having a green card, officially known as a Permanent Resident Card, would allow Sami and Eman to live and work permanently here. However, qualifying for a green card can be a challenge and could take years. The employer-based category, which Eman would qualify for, limits the number of green cards available each year for people whose job skills are needed in the US market and who offer skills that an employer cannot find from the local market of US workers. In most cases, a job offer is required before the immigrant can seek a green card. In addition, the burden of application is on the employer, who must begin and actively participate in the process. It can be an expensive process with no guarantee of success. President Trump's plan to limit the H-1B even more had ratcheted up anxiety levels and created uncertainty for Eman and many other skilled workers in the United States. "We've heard of another option," she said. "It's immigration to Canada where you can quickly get employment permits." Evidently Canada's year-old Global Skills Strategy program offers work permits similar to America's H-1B visa. In Canada, Eman and Sami could also apply for permanent residence, which might take as little as six months.

Insecurity about the future has been a consistent part of the family's life in the United States. Any decision they make is like parachuting off an airplane in a windstorm with no idea where they will land.

"I'm frustrated and exhausted with continually having to think about our future. All I want is to live a stable life full of hope and energy," she said.

On only a few occasions had I seen that hope wane, but it always surfaced again as she related her life stories in our interviews. As I took a last sip of my tea, I realized that this would be my final formal conversation with Eman. I had been privileged not only to hear and write about her life but also to actually participate in it. It allowed me to observe the coming alive of memories and emotions and to see the power of finding meaning in life. I was uplifted by the discoveries that Eman made along the way. I thanked her for allowing me to be part of her story.

"And what about you, Eman?" I asked. "We've talked for more than two years and you've read through the draft of the book. What are your thoughts about telling your story?"

She took a sip of the tea she had neglected, opened the cover of the notebook that contained a copy of the Eman section, and riffled through the double-spaced pages. After thinking for a few minutes, she said, "I already knew that my faith in Allah was a huge factor in my success, and when I thought deeply about many things that happened in my life, I could see there was something good in every struggle even if I didn't realize it right away. These were the discovery moments when I would wake up and understand something more." With her hand still on the open notebook, she paused for a minute with her eyes closed. I withheld my usual response to fill the silence with another question. Then she continued. "Sometimes recalling the past was a bit painful, but I learned from it. Being able to read my story in print has made me much stronger. It has given me some positive energy and feedback about myself."

She looked down at the notebook again and turned to the map of Libya on the first page. Putting her fingertip on the map, she outlined the border of her country and rested it on Tarhuna where she was born. If this dot on the map had come alive, she would have embraced it.

"Living abroad has made me love Libya so much more. It's my home, my huge mother." With a catch in her throat, she continued, "It's generosity… hospitality…a kind of purity." The emotion of her words surprised her. She stopped for a moment with her hand on her mouth and then added, "I pray for Libya."

"I'm sorry, Connie. Sometimes I don't realize how strongly I feel."

She closed the notebook and took a deep breath. "Reading about myself proves to me that I've learned to be tough and overcome feelings of sadness and frustration in order to keep going. I'm so thankful for my grandmother, my parents, and every member of my family. I pray that Allah will reward them."

Although our conversations have come to an end, my relationship with Nisren and Eman will continue. Their stories have nourished me and, hopefully, empowered them. Immersing myself in their life stories has been a bonding ritual that has shattered illusions of our differences and given me a deep sense of how similar we are. Knowledge of people different from us can erase the suspicion that engenders fear and, in turn, enables stereotypes and hatred. Only a small number of Muslims live in America, only one percent, so it is not surprising many Americans may never have had a Muslim friend or neighbor. It is my hope that becoming acquainted with the life stories of Nisren and Eman will help to bridge the gap between us and them with the realization that there is only us.

Acknowledgments

MY LONG JOURNEY TO WRITING *TASTE THE SWEETNESS* HAS BEEN ENCOURAGED BY MANY PEOPLE AND EVENTS. It started in Cairo, Egypt, when my husband, Floyd, accepted a position at American University in Cairo with the goal of initiating a new M.A. program in Mass Communication. I thank Floyd for providing not only an exciting turning point in my life but also for enriching the lives of our children: Troy, Melissa, and Sonja. From childhood to their grown-up lives, they have filled me with pride as they demonstrated their openness and friendship to people of other cultures and nationalities. Their spouses Diana, Mark, and Pambos and my grandchildren, Loucas, Antony, and Socratis in Cyprus and Benjamin, Kayla, and Jesslyn here in Colorado have followed in their parents' footsteps.

The four years we spent in Cairo ignited my interest in the Middle East and Muslim women. I thank my friend Dr. Shahinaz Talaat, Cairo University professor, for inspiring me with her courage, academic achievements and belief in freedom of expression. Another inspiration during the American University years was Dr. Jehan Sadat, now in the US, who devoted her life to human rights and improving the status of women in Egypt. A lucky chain of events after our return from Cairo changed my professional life. I was awarded a fellowship from The Rocky Mountain Women's Institute to begin writing *Seven Egyptian*

Women on the campus of Colorado Women's College in Denver. In turn, this led to the invitation to join Bridge International Language Center on the same campus and on to the founding of Spring Institute for International Studies.

Throughout my teaching, administrative, and consulting career, I have become well acquainted with other Muslim women who have informed me about different aspects of Islam and its role in their lives. My appreciation goes to three women in particular; Shareefa Al Said, Oman, who gave me insight into Ibadi Islam and her life as a member of the royal family; Guliz Mehmet, Turkish Republic of Cyprus, who brought fun, love of family, and a more secular view to my perspective, and Summer Kamber, United Arab Emirates, who courageously faced many difficulties by relying on the best of two religions. Thank you also to Dr. Mark Clarke whose referrals involved me in a return to Egypt to participate in a USAID evaluation of English language teaching and a visit to Tunisia with teammate Susan Polycarpou to offer writing workshops for high school teachers. Dr. Leyah Malcha Bergman-Lanier, director of SILC at the University of Arkansas Fayetteville, gave me the opportunity to team up with her on an AmidEast Bi-Communal Support Program in the Turkish Republic of Northern Cyprus. This project introduced me to journalists, business people, attorneys, and government employees who required English language skills to better communicate with Greek Cypriots. While teaching English to men and women students from every Muslim majority country and other nations in the world, I have learned important life lessons about the goodness and humanity of individuals from all cultural backgrounds.

This book would not have been written without the inspiration of my colleagues at Spring International Language Center (SILC) and, in actuality, I would not have been involved as a founder of Spring without my husband's support when we began Spring Institute for

International Studies in 1979 with Barbara and Bob Sample and Pambos Polycarpou, who encouraged me in publication of my first ESL textbook. My valued colleagues include Shirlaine Castellino, Director of SILC Littleton, who has offered support and encouragement in all of my retirement projects. Former colleagues who have inspired me with their dedication to SILC's students and continue to offer their skills to immigrants, refugees, and international students are Jeanne Hind, retired director of Spring International Denver, Marty Dawley, Gerre Shenkin, Karen Caddoo, Cheryl Kaas, Janet Ludwig, Karen Allred-Dennis, Patricia Cate, Peggy Solomon, Parmelee Welsh, and Bonnie Wetherbee. My thanks also to former staff members Darlene Steinle, Nicole Esteve, and Helen Jackman.

An important part of SILC's mission has been the belief in encouraging the language acquisition and personal progress of students through an atmosphere of support, openness, and understanding. Current faculty and staff continue to inspire met as I see them carry on these beliefs. Melissa Hull, Community Outreach Coordinator, successfully continues the host family and Conversation Partners programs that have involved the Littleton community for almost forty years. As my daughter, she has also cheered on my writing and willingly serves as my chief book promoter. My gratitude also to the present faculty and staff of SILC, who have energized my writing of Taste: Andy Pulford, assistant director; Tom Rohrbach, who is always there to offer a joke and to solve my computer glitches; Debby McBride, administrative assistant; Kristen Breaux and Ashley McBride, foreign student advisors, and Khiria Ali, office assistant, who represent Spring's friendliness and caring in their positions in the front office; and to instructors Colleen McGovern, Kristine Miller, Constance Lederer, Susan Blahut, Anne Lanctot, and Mari Hardy. More recent additions to the staff from the Denver center of SILC continue to embody the ideals of excellence in instruction and care and concern for international students.

Shari Caudron, writing coach and Light House Writers instructor gave me the impetus I needed to complete *The Good Daughter: Secrets, Life Stories, and Healing* and offered wise insight into the structure of *Taste the Sweetness*. She also led me to Cindi Yaklich, Epicenter Creative, the cover and interior designer of the book. Susan Polycarpou provided a keen eye, cultural sensitivity and expert advice in early drafts of Taste the Sweetness. Anne Lanctot, SILC instructor, waltzed professionally through the Chicago style manual as she copy-edited and proofed the final manuscript.

Other companions on the last lap of my journey to this book include the hard-working board members of Immigrant Pathways Colorado (IPC), formerly the Immigrant Integration Initiative (LI3). They have inspired me with their dedication to providing individual grants to immigrants and refugees for education, citizenship fees, tools for trade, and more.

My belief in the power of telling and writing life stories has been strengthened by the participants in the memoir classes I teach for Osher Life Long Learning (OLLI) sponsored by the University of Denver. These wise, experienced men and women have discovered the "a-ha" moments in their lives and willingly shared them with class members. Congratulations go to Patricia Ann Paul, a former class member who just recently published her memoir *Curse of Interesting Times: A Vietnam-Era Memoir*.

What could I do without the sounding board and stimulation of the Open Minds discussion group? You have tolerated all my allusions to the Arab world and Muslim interests and offered generosity to immigrants. Former group member Manijeh Badiozamani, who is completing her memoir, *Family Tales from Teheran and Other Short Stories*, has been a great friend and supporter of my writing plus giving me insight into shared teachings of Islam and Christianity.

ACKNOWLEDGMENTS

And, finally, my arrival at the *Taste the Sweetness* destination was made possible by Nisren and Eman, who have entrusted me with their amazing life stories.

Discussion Questions

1. As Kurds, Nisren and her family were in a minority in Iraq. How did this affect their daily lives?

2. How did the U.S. invasion of Iraq change their lives?

3. Saddam Hussein and Muammr Qaddafi were two powerful dictators. What characteristics did they share?

4. What does "eyes are on us" mean? In what ways did these "eyes" control Iraqi and Libyan citizens?

5. Both Nisren and Eman are Muslim, one Shiia and one Sunni. Did you see any differences in their beliefs or practice of their religion?

6. What religious and cultural customs did they observe in the engagement and wedding process?

7. What part did fear play in the women's lives? Have you ever experienced similar fears?

8. What strengths do each of these women have? Where did they get their strength? How did they use it?

9. Homesickness was one of the major difficulties Nisren and Eman experienced. Was this yearning for family and country ever eased? If so, how? What experiences have you had with homesickness?

DISCUSSION QUESTIONS

10. Culture shock added to their homesickness. What were the cultural differences that surprised them the most?

11. What individual hopes did each woman have for their families' futures in America?

12. "Swallow it now and you'll taste the sweetness later" was advice given to Eman by her grandmother. How did each of the women's lives demonstrate this saying?

13. America is a country divided by race, religion, ethnicity, and political party. Is it possible to bridge that gap to unite as one people? If so, how? How can we help new Americans to fully participate and feel part of our society?

ABOUT THE AUTHOR

Connie Shoemaker's interest in Muslim women began during her family's four years in Cairo, Egypt, where she taught English as a foreign language at American University in Cairo and wrote for the Associated Press. More than half her life has been focused on education of international students and immigrants. She is co-founder and director emerita of Spring International Language Center and serves on the board of Immigrant Pathways Colorado.

CPSIA information can be obtained
at www.ICGtesting.com
Printed in the USA
FSHW022057110920
73735FS